Shakespeare in Theory

Shakespeare in Theory
The Postmodern Academy and
the Early Modern Theater

Stephen Bretzius

Ann Arbor

The University of Michigan Press

For Maya,
the only begetter

Copyright © by the University of Michigan 1997
All rights reserved
Published in the United States of America by
The University of Michigan Press
Manufactured in the United States of America
♾ Printed on acid-free paper
2000   1999   1998   1997   4   3   2   1

A CIP catalog record for this book is available
from the British Library.

Library of Congress Cataloging-in-Publication Data

Bretzius, Stephen, 1956–
    Shakespeare in theory : the postmodern academy and the early
modern theater / Stephen Bretzius.
        p.   cm.
    Includes bibliographical references and index.
    ISBN 0-472-10853-0 (cloth : acid-free paper)
    1. Shakespeare, William, 1564–1616—Criticism and interpretation—
History—20th century. 2. Shakespeare, William, 1564–1616—Study
and teaching (Higher)—United States. 3. English drama—Early
modern and Elizabeth, 1500–1600—History and criticism—Theory, etc.
4. English drama—Early modern and Elizabethan, 1500–1600—Study
and teaching (Higher)—United States. 5. Postmodernism (Literature)
I. Title.
PR2970.B74   1997
822.3'3—dc21   97-33787
                                                            CIP

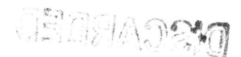

The word "theory" stems from the Greek verb *theorein*. The noun belonging to it is *theoria*. Peculiar to these words is a lofty and mysterious meaning. The verb *theorein* grew out of the coalescing of two root words, *thea* and *horao*. *Thea* (cf. theater) is the outward look, the aspect, in which something shows itself. . . . The second root word in *theorein*, *horao*, means: to look at something attentively, to look it over, to view it closely. Thus it follows that *theorein* is *thean horan*, to look attentively on the outward appearance wherein what presences becomes visible and, through such sight—seeing— to linger with it.

> —Martin Heidegger, "Science and Reflection"

Hamlet: 'Sblood, there is something in this more than natural, if philosophy could find it out. *A flourish.*

Guildenstern: There are the players.

> —*Hamlet*, 2.2.366–68

Acknowledgments

A book about the university and the theater is bound to have a number of supporting roles to acknowledge—and a few leading ones. Parts of this book began as dissertation work in Comparative Literature at Harvard University, and all of it owes a considerable debt to my thesis director, Barbara Johnson, as well as to insightful faculty like Harry Levin, G. Blakemore Evans, Walter Kaiser, Stanley Cavell, Alice Jardine, Marjorie Garber, Claudio Guillén, and Fredric Jameson. An earlier version of the chapter on *Othello* appeared in *Diacritics* (Spring 1987). An earlier version of "Synchronic Theory and Absolutism" first appeared in *Responses: On Paul de Man's Wartime Journalism*, edited by Werner Hamacher, Neil Hertz, and Thomas Keenan by permission of the University of Nebraska Press. Copyright © 1989 by the University of Nebraska Press. A version of chapter 3 was published in *College Literature* (Summer 1995) and portions of chapters 1 and 2 appeared as "Dr. Jacques L. and Martin Hide-a-Guerre: The Subject of New Historicism" in *Diacritics* (Spring 1997). Various chapters have benefited from comments by Heather Dubrow, Michael Riffaterre, Jonathan Culler, Geoffrey Hartman, Edward Pechter, Henry Sullivan, Susan Waldorf, Timothy Dalton, Nicola Watson, Dana Spradley, Marshall Brown, John Shoptaw, and others. A special thanks to my folks for all those editorial excursions to Palm Springs. The staff at the University of Michigan Press has also been immensely helpful, particularly LeAnn Fields, as have readers for the press. Thanks are due as well to Rob Wilson and the "theory group" at the University of Hawaii, to the surreal seminars of Joel Fineman at Berkeley, to Michael Fixler and John Fyler at Tufts, and to the Louisiana State University early modern contingent of Joe Ricapito, Don Moore, Larry Sasek, Ward Parks, and Kevin Cope. This book is also dedicated to Stephen Booth, because no one has seen further into Shakespeare, and to the memory of the immeasurably kind and wise Josephine Roberts.

Contents

Introduction

"Thou art a scholar, speak to it, Horatio," Marcellus cries at first sight of the Ghost in *Hamlet*, and with good reason.[1] For when Plato founded the first "academe" some time in the late 380s B.C.E. his mentor Socrates had already drawn the line dividing the twin faculties of literature and philosophy in strikingly similar terms. "First of all," he proscribes in the *Republic*, "the doings of Kronos, and the sufferings which in turn his son inflicted upon him, even if they were true, ought certainly not to be lightly told to young and thoughtless persons; if possible, they had better be buried in silence."[2] For Socrates, certain verse leads to vice, and vice versa, but from the beginning ("First of all") philosophy represses a violence whose return in *Hamlet* returns as well to a university already overrun, like the Wittenberg of Marlowe's *Doctor Faustus*, by theater.

This "haunting" of philosophy by *Hamlet* therefore offers a good place to begin *Shakespeare in Theory: The Postmodern Academy and the Early Modern Theater*, for each of the following chapters proposes that postmodern criticism performs the same cultural work as the early modern plays to which it increasingly refers. As the state to the stage so, for example, the White House to the ivory tower. This book also proposes that Shakespeare's centrality to a wide array of sometimes competing and contradictory postwar critical paradigms emerges itself as one more effect or consequence of this larger institutional displacement, from the early modern theater to the postwar, postmodern university. The title *Shakespeare in Theory* thus carries a double meaning, naming both the postwar academy's ongoing theoretical appropriation of Shakespeare (Shakespeare in theory) and the shaping influence of Shakespeare in, or within, literary theory. Indeed, what Steven Mullaney has said of "the place of the stage" in Elizabethan England may be said of the postmodern academy, whose "ivory tower" aloofness carries it, like the theater, outside the city walls but whose various disciplines, again like the theater, crisscross the entire fabric of that social order in all its variety and contradiction. As Mullaney observes of the theater, "the inscription of ideological values on civic space, the ritual creation of the social topology, did not halt at the boundary of the city walls. . . . The margins of the city were themselves a crucial part of its symbolic economy, but they served as a more ambivalent staging ground, as a place where the contradictions of the community—its incontinent hopes, fears, and desires—were prominently and dramatically set on stage."[3]

Traditionally, of course, the theater and the university serve distinct functions, the one performing and the other paraphrasing "knowledge." Nevertheless, the two institutions also share a history that reaches back to and through Plato's founding of his "academe." For more than thirty years before, in 423 B.C.E., Aristophanes had already comically established an imaginary "Thinkery" (*Phrontisterion*) for Socrates in *The Clouds.* So great was the effect created by this play, Leo Strauss suggests in *Socrates and Aristophanes*, that "one can easily receive the impression that Plato and Xenophon presented their Socrates in conscious contradiction to Aristophanes' presentation."[4] Intensifying Plato's "ancient disagreement of poetry and philosophy," both his *Apology* and *Phaedo* attempt to link Socrates' tragic fate to Aristophanes' burlesque.[5] "I do not know and cannot tell the names of my accusers," Socrates tells his audience-like jury of 501, "unless in the chance case of a comic poet."[6] For Walter Benjamin, Plato's account of Socrates' death represents "a parody of tragedy" in which one institutional discourse (theater) is sacrificed for the other (philosophy):

> Here, as often, the parody of a form proclaims its end. [Ulrich von] Wilamowitz testifies to the fact that it meant the end of tragedy for Plato. "Plato burnt his tetralogy; not because he was renouncing the ambition to be a poet in the sense of Aeschylus, but because he recognized that the tragedian could no longer be the teacher and master of the nation. He did of course attempt—so great was the power of tragedy—to create a new art form of tragic character, and he created a new cycle of legend to replace the obsolete heroic legends, the legend of Socrates."[7]

As Julia Reinhard Lupton and Kenneth Reinhard remark of this passage, "the scene of Socrates' death, staged quite literally as the tragedy to end all tragedy, structurally preserves tragic drama as precisely the unconscious of philosophical self-consciousness, the eclipsed signifiers of cultural origination whose cancellation underwrites the objects of philosophical reflection."[8]

The first university, in these terms, refashions and even represses a theater whose return at full force to the university in *Doctor Faustus* literally transforms the language of the university ("metaphysics") back into that of the theater ("magic"). In fresh receipt of his own controversial masters degree from Cambridge, Marlowe not only looks back to the early dramatized debates of John Heywood, which recast Platonic dialogue as dramatic dialogue, but more immediately looks ahead to Shakespeare's own notorious institutional variance of the theater and the university, as Richard Helgerson presents it:

> The persistent concern with status which marked virtually every response to the theater in the 1590s focused with particular intensity on Shakespeare. The "upstart crow" of the early 1590s, he was the darling of fools and gulls in the Parnassus plays of 1600 and 1601. As the player-poet who presented the most direct competition to the scholar-poets at their own specialty of producing artful and learned theatrical texts, the player-poet who could "bombast out a blank verse" with the best of them, Shakespeare became an indigestible lump in the craw of the authors' theater. He had either to be swallowed or spat up, assimilated as an author or rejected as a player. . . . Whatever the institutional constraints and contradictions that marked the 1590s, they worked themselves out in the particular experience of this ambitious, sensitive, and supremely talented man.[9]

Among Shakespeare's plays of the 1590s *Love's Labour's Lost* literally transforms the king of Navarre's would-be "academe"—"Our court shall be a little academe, / Still and contemplative in living art" (1.1.13–14)—into theater (the Pageant of the Nine Worthies). But in *Hamlet* perhaps most of all the logic-bound language of Faustus's Wittenberg gives way to the unlimited semiosis of Hamlet's bookish "There are more things in heaven and earth, Horatio, / Than are dreamt of in your philosophy" (1.5.166–67). For Benjamin the death of the theater and its rebirth as philosophy converge in Socrates, but they also converge, he goes on to suggest, in Hamlet:

> This age succeeded (at least once) in conjuring up the human figure who corresponded to this [Socratic] dichotomy between the neo-antique [tragic] and the medieval [philosophic] light in

which the baroque saw the melancholic. But Germany was
not the country which was able to do this. The figure is Hamlet. (157)

So in *King Lear*, Benjamin might allow, one institutional discourse
(philosophy) literally refigures the other (theater) at an equally crucial
juncture not just for the play but for the theater. For, set in a properly
prehistoric Albion, and at the furthest possible remove, in the literature of the West, from Platonic rationalism, the play itself goes mad
when the unprecedented heath scene draws to a close by turning into
just this inverted dialogue, now monologue, of the mad king's final
ramblings: "First let me talk with this philosopher. What is the cause
of thunder?"; "I'll talk a word with this same learnèd Theban. / What
is your study?"; "Noble philosopher, your company"; "With him; / I
will keep still with my philosopher"; "Come, good Athenian"
(3.4.154–84).

In postwar criticism, finally, a still more radical disruption of the
language of the university by the language of the theater begins with
Shakespeare's oft-noted influence on the two principal antecedents of
that criticism, Freud and Marx. In psychoanalysis Shakespeare represents the oedipal father from whom Freud first wrestles his oedipal
theory and to whom so many of his later writings return. For Marx,
too, Shakespeare exerts an almost equally pronounced influence, as
Eleanor Marx affirms in a brief remembrance of her father:

> Mohr [Marx] also read aloud to his children. To me, as to my
> sisters, he read the whole of Homer, the *Niebelungenlied*,
> Gudrun, *Don Quixote, The Thousand and One Nights.*
> Shakespeare was our family Bible, and before I was six I knew
> whole scenes from Shakespeare by heart.[10]

Not only is Marx's family Bible Shakespeare, but his family name,
Mohr (the Moor), holds up Shakespeare's emblem of repressive multinational enslavement—the Moor—as Marx's own (the proletariat's
own) "alter ego." Against a shared Shakespearean backdrop Marx's
family drama in London replays Freud on Shakespeare the way Freud's
1939 flight to London replays Marx.

In the postwar academy, then, a corresponding historical and psychological backdrop for the criticism already situates the theory
within a larger ideological and institutional theater, as Jacques Derrida
observes of the following comments from Kant's treatise "The
Conflict of the Faculties":

It must be said that the organizing of a university, with respect to its classes and faculties, was not just a matter of chance, but that the government, without showing any special wisdom or precocious knowledge for doing so, was, from a particular need that it felt (for influencing the people through various teachings), able to fasten *a priori* upon a principle of division that harmonizes happily [*glücklich*] with the principle currently in force.[11]

According to Derrida:

[The university] is authorized [*berechtigt*] by a non-university agency—here, by the state—and according to criteria no longer necessarily or finally those of scientific competence, but those of a certain performativity. . . . Regarding this power, university autonomy is in a situation of heteronomy, an autonomy conferred and limited, a representation of autonomy—in the double sense of representation by delegation and a theatrical representation. (6)

In Derrida's view Mallarmé's Hamletism epitomizes the irreducible "performativity" of Michel Foucault's "theatrum philosophicum," but, as Derrida himself contends in a later essay on "Deconstruction is/in America," so does deconstruction: "I have noticed this, so late, too late, as if by a contretemps. *Hamlet* in fact haunts the book I have just written, *Specters of Marx.*"[12] In an interview a few years before with Derek Attridge, Derrida remarks: "I would very much like to read and write in the space or heritage of Shakespeare, in relation to whom I have infinite admiration and gratitude; I would like to become (alas, it's pretty late) a 'Shakespeare expert'; I know that everything is in Shakespeare: everything and the rest, so everything or nearly."[13]

To be sure, other authors beyond Shakespeare—Milton, Wordsworth, Goethe, Hugo, Emerson, Mallarmé, Woolf, Joyce—strongly shape the language of postwar criticism and theory through Marx, Freud, and beyond. Yet each of these authors, it may also be said, offers versions of Emerson's somewhat exemplary depiction of Shakespeare the ghostwriter: "Now literature, philosophy and thought are Shakespearized. His mind is the horizon beyond which, at present, we do not see"—Joyce's "Maistre Sheames de la Plume . . . was . . . aware of no other shaggspick, other Shakhisbeard . . . as he was himself."[14] Even in the earliest years of postwar criticism, a similar Shakespearean horizon already gives a name to Cleanth Brooks's landmark new critical study, *The Well-Wrought Urn* (1947):

> The urn to which we are summoned, the urn which holds the ashes of the phoenix, is like the well-wrought urn of Donne's "Canonization" which holds the phoenix-lovers' ashes: it is the poem [Shakespeare's "Phoenix and the Turtle"] itself.[15]

For Paul Stevens, Brooks's appeal to the purely formal dimensions of paradox and irony not only corroborates widespread charges of critical "quietism" but also rewrites a specifically Renaissance literature into a decidedly postmodern criticism:

> When the Southern intellectuals were assimilated into the academy as the New Critics, not only were they displacing their conservatism into the study of literature and reinforcing the Arnoldian quietism of the discipline, but in persuading so many to idealize paradox, "the wisdom of untruths or double truths," they were idealizing their own cultural origins, and more important, drawing the rest of us into the strange act of veneration. In this, and to the extent to which we are willing to let paradox mask self-interest, we prove ourselves the heirs of not only Sir Thomas Brown and John Donne, but also Samuel Purchas and George Donne.[16]

However paradoxical or ironic the charges, a corresponding early modern context for postmodern criticism also characterizes the interplay of theater and theory at issue in each of the following chapters, an inter-play itself played out across a wide spectrum of contemporary critical movements and methodologies: the new historicism, psychoanalysis, multiculturalism, feminism, pragmatism, deconstruction, and nuclear criticism. In each instance the place of the university gives a local habitation and a name to the plays of the early modern theater, philosophy with everything Socrates rules out—the Ghost itself—in rule. A final chapter on "Shakespeare and the Beatles" extends the question of Shakespeare's influence to the postwar university's larger place in postmodern culture and to that culture's equally overdetermined relation to the poetry and drama.

The theater and the university thus share significant common ground in and around Shakespeare, but, as Helgerson emphasizes, the two institutions are also uniquely, even notoriously, distinct or separate. In their day many of the plays had probable early or first performances at Cambridge, Oxford, and the various Inns of Court; today these same plays are most frequently performed in university theaters and debated in classrooms. The generation of playwrights immediately preceding Shakespeare—and whom, as "upstart Crow," he controversially supersedes—has come to be called "University Wits." During these same early years of the theater Shakespeare himself may have been a schoolmaster. Yet among all Renaissance dramatists, and even among all writers, Shakespeare also represents the single most irreducible difference within or between the theater and the university, since his very identity as author has been repeatedly denied—and often by established academicians—in large part because he never attended the university. His most conspicuous pretender, the seventeenth earl of Oxford, records in the title "Oxford" a similar institutional bias, as if the plays and poetry were necessarily the result of university training. Today, I consider, the wheel has come full circle, and, whereas the early modern theater once usurped the university, the postmodern university now refashions the theater, recasting in a theoretical register the same disappearing subjects, the same ideological contradictions, and the same imperialist illusions that it uncovers in Shakespeare.

The Subject of New Historicism

In setting forth Shakespeare's unique role within an important institutional appropriation of the early modern theater by the postmodern university, the new historicism is a good place to begin. For the critical movement or school not only rewrites, in both its earliest and most concentrated forms of critical expression, the language of the first institution into the language of the second, the theater into the theory, but also deconstructively subjects its own ongoing critique to the institutional, cultural, and representational forces that it uncovers in the literature, and above all in Shakespeare. As one of the methodology's principal practitioners, Louis Montrose, observes, "integral to this new project of historical criticism is a realization and acknowledgment that the critic's own text is as fully implicated in such an interplay [of history and representation] as are the texts under study; a recognition of the agency of criticism in constructing and delimiting its object of study, and of the historical positioning of the critic vis-à-vis that object."[1] In still more recent remarks from an essay entitled "New Historicisms" (1992), Montrose revises and expands this particular institutional, ideological, and conceptual *mise-en-abyme:*

> Integral to any genuinely new-historicist project . . . must be a realization and acknowledgment that our analyses necessarily proceed from our own historically, socially, and institutionally shaped vantage points and that the pasts we reconstruct are, at the same time, the textual constructs of critics who are, ourselves, historical subjects. . . . It also becomes necessary to historicize the present as well as the past, and to historicize the dialectic between them—those pressures by which the past has shaped the present and the present reshapes the past. Such a critical practice constitutes a dialogue between a *poetics* and a *politics* of culture.[2]

For Montrose the object of any historical critique necessarily includes the critique. To what extent, then, does the new historicism itself localize in the postmodern university the very historical, cultural, and subjective forces played out in the early modern theater, to which it is therefore (and even new-historically) beholden?

In thus offering a properly new-historicist account of the new historicism, both with regard to its preoccupation with Shakespeare and insofar as it represents, today, a prevailing institutional critique of the institution and of a certain historicist approach to literary studies generally, I want to consider two essays by another of the movement's most representative critics, Stephen Greenblatt. The first is "Psychoanalysis and Renaissance Culture," a reading of Martin Guerre and Shakespearean drama, and the second is "Shakespeare and the Exorcists," a reading of *King Lear.* In the case of Martin Guerre, his true-life story, retold most recently in Natalie Zemon Davis's *The Return of Martin Guerre* and in a French film of the same name, is perhaps well known: how, in 1548, Martin quarrels with his father and suddenly abandons his home, wife Bertrande, son Sanxi, and patrimony; how, several years later, he returns—or, rather, an impostor claiming to be Martin returns, one Arnaud du Tilh, alias Pansette (the Belly), who assumes Martin's home, wife Bertrande, son Sanxi, and patrimony; and, finally, years later, how Martin himself returns, on a wooden leg, wounded in the Dutch wars, just at the moment when the court of Toulouse seems ready to pronounce Arnaud du Tilh the real Martin Guerre, this in response to a suit brought by Martin's uncle alleging deception. A new trial is called, and Arnaud is found guilty of imposture, hanged, and burned.

In "Psychoanalysis and Renaissance Culture" Greenblatt tells his version of the story. Here, too, there are two Martins, as there are two stories: a Martin Guerre of psychoanalysis, held up in the traffic of personal and biological drives and memory traces explored by Freud, and a Martin Guerre of historicism, the placeholder in a web of anonymous cultural and institutional practices. In Greenblatt's version, where the Freudian subject is Martin and the historical subject Arnaud, the impostor is clear *from the beginning* and quickly unmasked. Psychoanalysis, representing the uncle, brings suit against Arnaud, but Greenblatt, returning for the nephew, is surprisingly clear on the question of priority and on the subject's relation to history: "Martin's [psychoanalytic] subjectivity—or, for that matter, Arnaud's or Bertrande's—does not any the less exist, but it seems peripheral, or rather, it seems to be the *product* of the relations, material objects, and judgments exposed in the case rather than the *producer* of these relations, objects, and judgments."[3] However deep their psychology, "these selves seem brought into being by the institutional processes set in motion by Arnaud's imposture" (137). Even Freud would need to acknowledge that Arnaud had passed for Martin by means of all the unconscious mechanisms of deception and resistance that, for Freud, already constitute the original. Martin is the one-legged subject of psychoanalysis, but Arnaud is its unconscious, a properly political unconscious whose drives and desires have more to do with the life of nations than of individuals. "In such a discursive system," Greenblatt concludes—but we must hear the door opening here, at the height of these closing remarks on naive psychologizings of the literary subject and on the authenticity of Arnaud, the primacy of process, as if Martin didn't have a leg to stand on *because* position is more, much more, than nine-tenths of the law—"In such a discursive system," Greenblatt concludes, "psychoanalytic interpretation seems to me crippled" (137).

"Crippled," then, invokes Martin's return at the precise moment when all he comes to represent—"the faith that the child is the father of the man and that one's days are bound each to each in biological necessity" (134)—disappears. Here, if only for a moment, the controlling dialectic of the new historicism, the displacement-as-return of "subversion," is its own. For at a moment like "crippled," the return of the repressed, strictly speaking, is the return of the repressed, psychoanalysis, but with a keen awareness that the difference between this loss and its return, what Freud labels castration, is more fundamentally a kind of *random* violence, the purely historical violence held in place by Martin's missing leg and which the latter carries with him like a name, his nom de guerre—the returning or prodigal son, then, *of* historical violence.

To see this, and to follow out now the institutional implications of this double subject for the new historicism, let us briefly consider the second essay by Greenblatt mentioned above, "Shakespeare and the Exorcists." Here Greenblatt frames his reading of *King Lear* with an account of Samuel Harsnett's *Declaration of Egregious Popish Impostures* (1603), which Shakespeare draws from in the play. Harsnett's tract attacks a group of exorcists led by the Jesuit William Weston, alias Father Edmunds. By exposing its essential theatricality, its "devill theatre," Harsnett wants to drive exorcism out of the kingdom. Instead, Greenblatt suggests, he drives it right into the playhouses. When Shakespeare draws from Harsnett's *Egregious Impostures* he literalizes a large cultural shift, one that confines a necessary ritual of possession within the carefully regulated limits of the national theater. "With this emptying out, Harsnett will have driven exorcism from the center to the periphery—in the case of London, quite literally to the periphery, where increasingly stringent urban regulation had already driven the public playhouses" (*Negotiations*, 176). From the frame narrative to the play, from Father Edmunds to Edmund, the cultural force of *King Lear* greatly eclipses that of Harsnett's *Declaration* not just because the play harnesses the tremendous social energies that made of possession a kind of living theater but because the action itself is possessed by this very *secularization*, "haunted by a sense of rituals and beliefs that are no longer efficacious, that have been emptied out" (177).

First published two years before Greenblatt's essay on Martin Guerre, "Shakespeare and the Exorcists" thus leaves off where "Psychoanalysis and Renaissance Culture" begins, with an account of the way *King Lear* survives the cultural conditions that produced it because "the play recuperates and intensifies our need for these ceremonies, even though we do not believe in them," satisfying "our desire for spectacular impostures" (183–84). Central to both essays is the notion of "possession," set against the uncanny resemblance between Harsnett's attempts to drive out exorcism and Greenblatt's attempts to displace psychoanalysis. Harsnett exposes exorcism for what it is, a living theater, something the essay on Martin Guerre implicitly proposes with respect to psychoanalysis and its own links to older rituals and myths of possession explored by Freud in *Totem and Taboo*, rituals and myths that seem to have a special persistence wherever the very orthodoxy of Freud's method is being invoked, as by Greenblatt, in order to be resisted, from Claude Lévi-Strauss's scattered comments on psychoanalysis and shamanism to Jacques Lacan's "it is as if a demon plays a game with our watchfulness" to Jacques Derrida's "mystic writing pad."[4] In the new historicism psychoanalysis is not just exposed as theater—the burden of the Martin Guerre essay—but performed, like Harsnett's exorcism, in theory, and at a time when rapid technological advances and global capitalist expansion would seem to make the embodied ego as obsolete for the later twentieth century as it proved for the later sixteenth. A deep and ongoing tension between natural and legal selves is only made unusually clear, for example, in something like the "Baby M" case, or the trial of Kimberly Mays, in which the rights of a natural mother were superseded by a contract. Against a cultural backdrop not so different from the one yielding Harsnett's exorcism of exorcism, as Greenblatt often suggests, the subject of psychoanalysis becomes the object of new historicism ("At issue is not Martin Guerre as subject but Martin Guerre as object" [136–37]). Whereas the entire spectrum of poststructuralist literary criticism—deconstruction, Marxism, feminism, semiotics, psychoanalysis itself—strategically develops, and in widely varying ways, the Freudian subject as a necessary and sometimes dangerous fiction, in the new historicism this emptying out is *performed*, in state-sponsored universities, its practitioners would say, rather than government-controlled playhouses (Greenblatt's "English professors are salaried, middle-class shamans" [*Negotiations*, 1]). As Montrose observes of the methodology's mix of older and newer historicisms, "it may well be that these very ambiguities rendered New Historicism less a critique of dominant critical ideology than a subject for ideological appropriation, thus contributing to its almost sudden installation as the newest academic orthodoxy, to its rapid assimilation by the 'interpretive community' of Renaissance literary studies."[5]

Reading the new historicism new-historically, the methodology does not just account for but recounts Martin's story. In Greenblatt's criticism of the 1980s the correspondingly close relation between the new historicism and its own critical and historical moment perhaps best characterizes an essay published in the same year as the essay on Martin Guerre (1986) and entitled "Towards a Poetics of Culture." For here the central example of such a poetics is provided by Michael Rogin's account "*Ronald Reagan*, the Movie" (1981), which Greenblatt conveniently summarizes:

> In a brilliant paper that received unusual attention, elicited a response from a White House speech-writer, and most recently generated a segment on CBS's "Sixty Minutes," the political scientist and historian Michael Rogin recently observed the number of times President Reagan has, at critical moments in his career, quoted lines from his own or other popular films. The President is a man, Rogin remarks, "whose most spontaneous moments—('Where do we find such men?' about the American D-Day dead; 'I am paying for this microphone, Mr. Green,' during the 1980 New Hampshire primary debate)—are not only preserved and projected on film, but also turn out to be lines from old movies."[6]

For Greenblatt, elaborating on Rogin's thesis, Ronald Reagan "is manifestly the product of a larger and more durable American structure—not only a structure of power, ideological extremism and militarism, but of pleasure, recreation, and interest, a structure that shapes the spaces we construct for ourselves, the way we present 'the news,' the fantasies we daily consume on television or in the movies" (154).

Extending "the fantasies we daily consume on television" to Rogin's own "Sixty Minutes" segment and "the way we present 'the news' " to, in this case, "the way we present the new historicism," the effect and even the intent here is partly to make Rogin's own historical criticism, like "Sixty Minutes" and like Ronald Reagan, a function or product of that same durable American structure. The projection of criticism onto history is complete when Greenblatt notes "the number of times President Reagan has, at critical moments in his career, quoted lines from his own and other popular films"—and then proceeds to quote these lines himself. This reel-to-real projection, in turn, almost literally characterizes Rogin's essay, insofar as the "Sixty Minutes" segment based on his research prompted more protest mail than any segment ever on the show, making Rogin's essay at once the most popular and unpopular contemporary critique of the Reagan myth. That it should be associated, methodologically and institutionally, with the new historicism (Rogin, like Greenblatt, helped found the journal *Representations* and teaches at the University of California at Berkeley) is, again, a tautology. For the stranger-than-truth story of "President Reagan" exemplifies Greenblatt's "poetics of culture" in large part because it brings to the surface, rather than describes or clarifies, the shaping influence of political authority on literary-historical criticism as it is developed and, from Reagan to Rogin, literalized in the new historicism (hence, again very broadly and still at the level of the proper name, "I am paying for this microphone, Mr. Greenblatt"). So situated, the California connection underwriting the three-part relation of "President Reagan," the new historicism, and Berkeley in Greenblatt's "Towards a Poetics of Culture" proves sufficiently straightforward as to scarcely need repeating, except perhaps that Greenblatt himself insists upon it in the very next example: "Let us consider, for example, not the President's Hollywood career but a far more innocent California pastime, a trip to Yosemite National Park" (154).

From the theater to the theory, the new historicism is thus "new" not for what it says but for what it does, recasting the early modern theater—and above all *Hamlet*—in the postmodern university. Quoting from the introduction to Greenblatt's *Shakespearean Negotiations* on its author's shift from essentialism to "something that seems at first far less spectacular: a subtle, elusive set of exchanges, a network of trades and trade-offs, jostling of competing representations, a negotiation between joint stock companies," a sympathetic Lars Engle cannot help adding: "this is clearly a view of a market economy at work, and I believe that *if we can set aside* Adam Smith's rationalized views of how markets function (to say nothing of Ronald Reagan's fantasies on the subject), the idea of the market and the invisible large economy on which it is a window offer the kind of general illumination of Shakespeare's work that justifies calling it a Shakespearean philosophy."[7] In *Cold War Criticism and the Politics of Skepticism* Tobin Siebers remarks of similar affinities between the new historicism and the methodology's own centralizing authority: "the most satisfying explanation is to embrace the irony that Reaganomics and Greenblatt's own intellectual odyssey share similar goals."[8] For Alan Sinfield "the sense of entrapment that fascinates new historicism—in theory, in textual instances, in the sense of its own political scope—is tellingly homologous with its own professional entrapment," an entrapment only deepened, rather than finally resolved, by the election of a Democratic president named Bill, for now the dialectic of subversion and containment through which the methodology came to institutional prominence must be itself subverted, and therefore sustained.[9] Autobiographically, then, and not just metacritically, Greenblatt's reference to Reagan's (and Rogin's) "I am paying for this microphone, Mr. Green" signals a displacement of the historical dialectic under discussion onto the discussion itself, as do related signature-effects in other essays—thus, in "Invisible Bullets," "the stance that seemed to come naturally to me as a green freshman in mid-twentieth-century America"; in "Martial Law in the Land of Cockaigne," "we could go on to look at other instances of the 'green woman' and the tainted man in Renaissance drama"; in "The Improvisation of Power," "to an envious contemporary like Robert Greene, Shakespeare seems a kind of green-room Iago"; in "Resonance and Wonder," "Thomas Greene, who has written a sensitive book on what he calls the 'vulnerable text.' . . ."[10] In "Psychoanalysis and Renaissance Culture" Martin Guerre, like Reagan, contains an anagram (or near anagram, again by the difference of a letter) of the same signature "Green."

Replaying, in these ways, the subjective dialectics of the early modern theater in the postmodern university, the new historicism stands in not only for psychoanalysis but for Shakespeare. The literature of the double is most identified with stories like *Dr. Jekyll and Mr. Hyde*, or Poe's "William Wilson," but it is in Shakespeare's poetry and drama, Greenblatt suggests in the essay on Martin Guerre, that this subject receives its first, or fullest, development; when speaking of Stevenson, one is already speaking of a double or stand-in for Shakespeare anyway ("Perhaps my dearest and best friend outside of Shakespeare is [Dumas's] D'Artagnan. I know not a more human soul, nor, in its way, a finer")—so too, for example, William Wilson's "Elizabethan house."[11] Challenges to Shakespeare's authorship from Baconists and others (including Freud) subject Shakespeare himself to the same charge of imposturing. In the following passage from Greenblatt's discussion of the Martin-like "suppose" or substitution, the "loss of personal moorings" again recalls the "loss of moorings" in Greenblatt's essay on *King Lear* (122) and in an earlier essay on the unmoored Othello:

> Renaissance drama is particularly rich in such versions [of Martin's story]. From the larcenous impersonation of the missing husband in John Marston's play *What You Will*, to the romantic impersonations in Beaumont and Fletcher's tragicomedies, from Perkin Warbek's regal pretensions in John Ford's play of the same name to the sleazy tricks of Ben Jonson's rogues. ("But were they gulled / With a belief that I was Scoto?" asks Volpone. "Sir," replies the parasite Mosca, "Scoto himself could hardly have distinguished" [2.2.34–36].) Above all there are instances of imposture and loss of personal moorings in Shakespeare: the buffoonery of the false Vincentio in *The Taming of the Shrew*, the geometry of the paired twins in *The Comedy of Errors*, the more impassioned geometry of *Twelfth Night*. Even when there is no malicious, accidental, or natural double, Shakespeare's characters are frequently haunted by the sense that their identity has been lost or stolen: "Who is it that can tell me who I am?" crieds [*sic*, the fold of telling and tale at issue here] the anguished Lear. And in the most famous of the tragedies, the ghost of Old Hamlet—"Of life, of crown, of queen at once dispatched"— returns to his land to demand that his son take the life of an impostor who has seized his identity.[12]

In *Hamlet* most of all, Claudius displaces Hamlet in much the way that Arnaud displaces Martin, and the new historicism, psychoanalysis (and the quarrel of nephew and uncle in Martin's story makes *Hamlet* doubly appropriate). Telling that story, the essay privileges the subject of Renaissance culture over the subject of psychoanalysis, but the latter, like Old Hamlet and like Martin, returns. Insofar as any marginalized subject remains, as Greenblatt shows in the plays, deeply constitutive of any centralizing authority, psychoanalysis functions for the new historicism in much the way that marginalized subjects—Falstaff, Shylock, Cressida—function in the plays. The double, again, is in the title, and it is roughly the same story: Psychoanalysis is Dr. Jekyll, and Renaissance Culture is Mr. Hyde. This double, in turn, does not just arise on the level of theme but of form, the way, to return for a moment to *Romeo and Juliet*, the opening Chorus's "Is now the two hours' traffic of our stage" (12) extends the play's obsessive doubling ("Two households, both alike in dignity" [1]) to the "two hours" it takes to perform (Hamlet's "look you how cheerfully my mother looks, and my father died within 's two hours" [3.2.127–28]). Thus, when Greenblatt rounds out his discussion of Martin's story and Shakespeare by noting how, "in the most famous of the tragedies, the ghost of Old Hamlet—'Of life, of crown, of queen at once dispatched'—returns to his land to demand that his son take the life of an impostor who has seized his identity," "Old" Hamlet is the "above all" subject of "new" historicism *because* he is the totemic father of Freud's ur-oedipal narrative.

Hamlet thus harnesses the enormous cultural, ideological, and conceptual energies shaping, and shaped by, the early modern theater, but so, in a kind of haunting, does the criticism, and perhaps "above all" the new historicism—"Psychoanalysis and Renaissance Culture," again, turned "Dr. Jacques L. and Martin Hide-a-Guerre." Autobiographically, in turn, Martin's story carries special significance for Greenblatt's criticism, in which it returns to the following anecdote about his father in the introduction to *Learning to Curse*:

> My father was named Harry J. Greenblatt; his cousin Joseph H. Greenblatt. But when the latter became a lawyer, he moved into the same building in which my father had his office, and he began to call himself J. Harry Greenblatt. . . . There were, as I grew up, endless stories about J. Harry—chance encounters in the street, confusions of identity that always seemed to work to my father's disadvantage. . . . But a few years before my father's death at 86, the rivalry and doubling took a strange twist: J. Harry Greenblatt was indicated [*sic*, the fold, again, of telling and tale] on charges of embezzlement; the charges were prominently reported in the newspapers; and the newspapers mistakenly printed the name of the culprit as Harry J. Greenblatt. . . . The confusion was awkward, but it had at least one benefit: it enabled my father to tell a whole new set of stories about himself and his double. (7)

This engaging story of doubles gives personal point to the changing letter, Harry J. and J. Harry, that elsewhere separates history and literature, and frame narrative and play, in Greenblatt's criticism—Harriot and Harry, in "Invisible Bullets"; Father Edmunds and Edmund, in the essay on *King Lear*; Reagan and Rogin, in "Towards a Poetics of Culture"; Greenblatt and Guerre, in "Psychoanalysis and Renaissance Culture"; Marie and Maria, in a reading of *Twelfth Night*; "Fiction and Friction," to quote the title of this last essay; and so on. In each case the new historicism is "new" in part because the absolutist authority generated by its defining dialectic arises no longer from history (notwithstanding the criticism's colonialist emphasis) but from language, as Shakespeare again exemplifies; to begin with, England did not conquer the world, English did. Following this subjective dialectic, then, to the letter, Greenblatt's anecdote of J. Harry Greenblatt is framed by a pair of still more personal narrative doublings. In the first he writes,

> my mother was generously fond of telling me long stories I found amusing about someone named Terrible Stanley, a child whom I superficially resembled but who made a series of disastrous life decisions—running into traffic, playing with matches, going to the zoo without telling his mother, and so on. Stanley was the "other" with a vengeance, but he was also my double, and my sense of myself seemed bound up with the monitory tales of his tragicomic fate. (6)

In the second such narrative the scene switches to the university and to "a period . . . when I could not rid my mind of the impulse to narrate my being":

> I was a student at Cambridge, trying to decide whether to return to America and go to law school or graduate school in English. "He's sitting at his desk, trying to decide what to do with his life," a voice—my voice, I suppose, but also not my voice—spoke within my head. . . . I was split off from myself, J. Harry to my Harry J. (or Terrible Stanley to my Stephen), in an unhappy reprise of my earlier sense of self as story. . . . It occurred to me that I might be going mad. When the voice left me, it did so suddenly, inexplicably, with the sound of something snapping. (8)

From J. Harry Greenblatt to Terrible Stanley to the "detached narrativizing voice," these three variations on Martin's story assume three distinct generic forms, the first comic ("had my father not possessed considerable comic gifts"), the second "tragicomic," and the third tragic ("an unhappy reprise of my earlier sense of self as story"). As in Martin's case, the tragedy is once again *Hamlet* (the ghostlike visitation, the English academic backdrop, the return of "the 'other' with a vengeance," "it occurred to me that I might be going mad," "trying to decide whether to return," and so on); as in *Hamlet*, too, the indecision is so wrenching—"whether to . . . go to law school or graduate school in English"—because the terms are so interchangeable, the letter of the law (Martin) turned the law of the letter (Arnaud). For from one institutional extreme (the university) to the other (the theater), and from Harry to Hamlet, what Greenblatt says of his father's many stories necessarily goes for his story, Greenblatt's story, too:

> my father's narrative impulse, we can say, was a strategic way . . . of reestablishing the self on the site of its threatened loss. But there was an underside to this strategy that I have hinted at by calling his stories obsessive. For the stories in some sense *were* the loss of identity which they were meant to ward off—there was something compulsive about them, as if someone were standing outside of my father and insisting that he endlessly recite his tales. (7)

Like the theater it reviews, then, the new historicism does not so much resolve as replay Martin's trial—"The People versus New Historicism." For as new-historicist critics like Leah Marcus, Steven Mullaney, and Eric Mallin affirm, "'localization,'" to quote Marcus, "is an idea we need to apply to ourselves as readers as well as to what we read. In the same way that we have begun to explore the 'local' circumstances that have shaped past critical efforts . . . we need to locate our own attempts at reading, or at least never lose awareness that our activity has local coordinates of its own."[13] At its most local, then, the self-fashioning dialectic central to the new historicism ultimately unites its various readings, as in Montrose's essay "The Elizabethan Subject and the Spenserian Text," in which the return of subversion to its containment extends to Greenblatt's own influence on Montrose's reading:

> For Greenblatt, "Renaissance self-fashioning" involves submission to an absolute power or authority situated at least partially outside the self, and "is achieved in relation to something perceived as alien, strange, or hostile"; this "alien is always constructed as a distorted image of the authority," and

the authority that is produced in the encounter between them "partakes of both the authority and the alien that is marked for attack" (*Renaissance Self-Fashioning,* 9). It will be obvious that in the fashioning of my own text, Greenblatt's has functioned as both the authority and an other. My disagreements with his admirable book arise within the shape of a shared project; his work has enabled mine. (308)

Here, as in the Elizabethan poetry and drama to which Montrose ultimately refers, there is subversion ("my disagreements with his admirable book"), only not for Montrose ("arise within the shape of a shared project"). Elsewhere Montrose takes issue with Greenblatt's reliance on a rigorously absolutist dialectic of subversion and containment as itself too absolute: "this is a compelling formulation but its suggestion of an absolute and totalistic structure of royal power . . . is questionable on both empirical and theoretical grounds" (330). Refashioning the authority under discussion in the discussion, Greenblatt's account of a "totalistic structure of royal power" is itself "compelling." Much more generally, the critical and finally institutional concept of "Renaissance self-fashioning" can be resisted, but such resistance, of course, is its supreme expression, self-fashioning itself. As Montrose notes a little later in the essay, "we could say, then, in response to Greenblatt's brilliant provocation, that one of the supreme pleasures available to the subject of power is to impose upon the fictions whose enforced acceptance signifies his subjection, the marks of his own subjectivity" (331). In "Greenblatt's brilliant provocation," *provocation* brilliantly captures the approach-avoidance nature of Montrose's relation to Greenblatt's criticism, while *brilliant* provocatively extends the light and lunar imagery of the Elizabethan poetry under discussion to its reception, further refashioning the early modern dialectic of "the authority and the alien" in the postmodern, post-Heideggerean dialectic of theater and theory.

In the final, one-sentence paragraph of "Psychoanalysis and Renaissance Culture" Greenblatt returns directly to the terms of his title: "With the idea of an origin that is only conferred upon one *at the end* of a series of actions and transactions, I return to the notion that psychoanalysis is the historical outcome of certain characteristic Renaissance strategies" (144; my italics). Psychoanalysis is displaced as "the historical outcome of certain characteristic Renaissance strategies," but Martin—and even MacArthur—are recalled in "I return." In its final sentence Greenblatt's reading "returns" to its original question: Is desire psychoanalytic or historical, a function of sexual difference or class struggle? For his part Shakespeare always leaves that answer suspended, and the question of the subject unresolved. "Who is it that can tell me who I am?" cries the anguished Lear, but even if "Lear's shadow" is correct he will never know for sure whether he is Lear's shadow or whether it is Lear's shadow who can tell him who he is. Old Hamlet "returns to his land to demand that his son take the life of an impostor who has seized his identity," but leaves behind, as Stephen Booth has underlined, "the undiscovered country, from whose bourn / No traveller returns."[14]

Joel Fineman's "Shakespeare's Will"

From his early, baroque investigations of comic and tragic doubling in "Fratricide and Cuckoldry: Shakespeare's Doubles" (1977) to his posthumous, Wildean explorations of *The Subjectivity Effect in Western Literary Tradition: Essays toward the Release of Shakespeare's Will* (1991), sometimes Joel Fineman seems like the Thersites of literary theory, but his real dream was to play Hamlet. In a way he probably played it only too well, of course, what with the "centripetal claustrophilia" and all.[1] Yet for Fineman, Greenblatt, or anyone else to represent the "Hamlet" of literary theory it would again be necessary to understand that theory as a kind of theater—or, still more essentially, to understand the American academy as a kind of national theater, sharing first with that theater the ineluctable canonicity of, say, Hamlet himself. The focus here, then, is no longer the new historicism proper except insofar as Fineman's work, and psychoanalysis generally, constitute the "Other," writ large, of that methodology's own institutional or topical self-fashioning (Greenblatt's "Joel Fineman's writing amuses, fascinates, alarms, and at times outrages me, makes me nervous, forces me to think about familiar texts in unfamiliar ways," but also Fineman's own "the literary exigencies that determine the ways in which Shakespeare writes his literary subjects not only write the medical texts that are supposed to have influenced Shakespeare but, in addition, so too, the 'Stephen Greenblatt' who in his turn will come to write about those medical texts").[2]

Before turning directly to Fineman's two books, their central thesis—namely, "that current thought works to transfer into a theoretical register a constelled set of literary themes, metaphors, motifs, that Shakespeare introduces into literature, in response to specific literary exigencies, at and as the beginning of the end of the Humanist Renaissance"—may be briefly illustrated by way of a highly stylized early play like *Romeo and Juliet*.³ For here, and from the beginning, the play unfolds outside (and therefore inside) the "deconstructed" binarisms characteristic of a certain poststructural literary theory generally—womb/tomb, light/dark, female/male, Capulet/Montague, waking/sleeping, all/nothing, lark/nightingale, love/hate, late/early, vice/virtue, poison/remedy, mercy/murder, wedding/funeral, dove/raven, fiend/angel, wolf/lamb, miss/mend, stand/stir, haste/destiny, and so on.⁴ Here the nonbinary language of the theater anticipates the "unlimited semiosis" of postmodern literary and cultural theory precisely by extending that nonbinary language to the opposition theater/theory, which the play also undermines. To cite only one particularly central example, literary criticism's ongoing concerns with the cultural and ritualistic origins of tragedy are not just explored but explained—theorized—by the play's self-conscious identification of Juliet as both "dove" ("So shows a snowy dove trooping with crows" [1.5.48], "Sitting in the sun under the dovehouse wall" [1.3.26–27]) and "lamb" ("Juliet! Fast, I warrant her, she. / Why, lamb! Why, lady!" [4.5.1–2]). In the Nurse's "Come Lammas Eve at night shall she be fourteen" (1.3.17), Lammas Eve (*hlaf*, loaf, bread; *maesse*, mass [hlammas]) further returns the theatrical experience of the play's "poor sacrifices" (5.3.318) to the Catholic mass, out of which Shakespeare's own tragic theater significantly evolves—Capulet's "God's bread, it makes me mad!" (3.5.176).⁵ Redoubling this Christian context for sacrifice, a seasonal parallel in the myth of Persephone stolen away by Pluto shows through Capulet's "Death lies on her like an untimely frost / Upon the sweetest flower of all the field" (4.5.28–29) and "O son, the night before thy wedding-day / Hath Death lain with thy wife" (35–36). Within the same ongoing theorization of the play's own theater the "pomegranate tree" in Juliet's "It was the nightingale, and not the lark . . . / Nightly she sings on yon pomegranate tree" (3.5.2–4) further joins Juliet to Persephone, Lady Capulet to Ceres, and "love-devouring death" (2.6.7) to Hades.

From the play to the theory, then, the postmodern university gives rise to influential critiques of performative discourse and its ritualistic origins in postsubjective (post-Lacanian) sacrifice, but so, in *Romeo and Juliet*, does the early modern theater. For the play, and not simply the theory, is already about the play—and autobiographical, from Montague's "Away from light steals home my heavy son, / And private in his chamber pens himself" (1.1.137–38) through Juliet's "Was ever book containing such vile matter / So fairly bound" (3.2.83–84) to Romeo's frantic "get me ink and paper" (5.1.25) and the Prince's final

"This letter doth make good the friar's words, / Their course of love, the tidings of her death" (5.3.286–87), which is exactly what the opening Chorus has promised ("The fearful passage of their death-marked love" [9]). The play turns into the letter and the letter, at that moment, into a suicide note. Still more autobiographically, the Nurse's "Susan and she (God rest all Christian souls!) / Were of an age. Well, Susan is with God" (1.3.17–19) quite plausibly alludes in its decidedly non-Italian "Susan" to Shakespeare's own daughter Susanna, who, born in 1583, would have been nearing fourteen at the time of the play's probable composition (1596–97)—hence, too, Mercutio's "Farewell, ancient lady. Farewell, lady, lady, lady" (2.4.143–44), which echoes the refrain of the ballad "Chaste Susanna," but also, just before Juliet's first meeting with Romeo at the Capulet ball, the Servingman's "Good thou, save me a piece of marchpane and, as thou loves me, let the porter let in Susan Grindstone and Nell" (1.5.8–9), which corresponds, more properly, to something like the play's *signature* (Grindstone/Shake-spear).

2

So cast, as the story of the play's own "rare Italian master, Julio Romano," to echo Fineman on *The Winter's Tale* (5.2.97), *Romeo and Juliet* offers an early instance of Fineman's contention that literary theory's own unprecedented philosophical investment in Shakespeare

> raises the possibility that current thought works to transfer into a theoretical register a constelled set of literary themes, metaphors, motifs, that Shakespeare introduces into literature, in response to specific literary exigencies, at and as the beginning of the end of the Humanist Renaissance. If so, it is possible that current theorizations are important not because they offer a method or even a point of view with which to look back at Shakespeare, but, instead, because they participate in the very same literary history within which Shakespeare writes his sonnets, emerging now as a symptomatic and epiphenomenal consequence of the way, at the beginning of the modernist epoch, Shakespeare rethinks the literature he succeeds. Putting the question more strongly, we can ask whether, repeating Shakespeare's repetition, it is possible for contemporary theory to do so with a difference. (*SW*, 113)

As one more "symptomatic and epiphenomenal consequence" of this discursive and institutional displacement, in each of Fineman's two books, *Shakespeare's Perjured Eye: The Invention of Poetic Subjectivity in the Sonnets* (1986) and *Shakespeare's Will* (1991), Oscar Wilde illustrates the shaping influence of Shakespeare's poetry and drama on the modernist (and psychoanalytic) subject. In the sonnet book, "Wilde's *The Portrait of Mr. W. H.* is the only genuinely literary criticism that Shakespeare's sonnets have ever received, and part of the reason for this circumstance is that, like Shakespeare's sonnets, it too is caught up in the literary problematic that derives from the effort to imagine a visible language."[6] In *The Importance of Being Earnest* Wilde further establishes " 'Jack-Ernest' as the only authentic revenant of Shakespearean 'Will' " ("My ideal has always been to love someone of the name of Ernest" [28]). For in the case of this particular conjunction of "visual deictic and verbal name," Fineman suggests, "Wilde's evacuating clarification of Shakespearean characterology, his 'Bunburying' of Shakespearean person, supports my argument that with their 'Will' Shakespeare's sonnets inaugurate and give a name to the modernist literary self, thereby specifying for the future what will be the poetic psychology of the subject of representation" (29). Inscribing, then, *eros* by any other name, even *arrows* (Cupid with his bow and *eros*), it is not so much Jack's "Earnestness," or even Oscar's "Wild," but Freud's "Pleasure Principle," Sigmund's *Freude,* that represents "the only authentic revenant of Shakespearean 'Will,' " from the "Fine-man" of verbal "rope-tricks," finally, to the "young man" of the visionary sonnets.

In *Shakespeare's Perjured Eye* Fineman seeks to make this relation to theory explicit, situating the invention of a novel and thoroughly literary subject in the deconstructive fold or difference between the ideal specularity of the young man sonnets ("that sun, thine eye") and the deflected difference introduced into this relation by the dark lady sonnets ("My mistress' eyes are nothing like the sun"). For Fineman, the second subsequence deconstructs the first but with this difference: "it is significant that Derrida's subsequent attempt to rupture Lacan's rupture, Derrida's putatively postsubjective account of supplemental *différance,* seems, from the point of view of Shakespeare's sonnets, nothing but another 'increase' that 'from fairest creatures we desire' (1)" (45). The play on *subsequent* ties Derrida's revision of Lacan into the second subsequence's revision of the first. When Fineman twice refers to the dark lady as "a species of the non-species" (176, 244), he refers as well to the close of Derrida's essay "Structure, Sign, and Play." But Fineman several times insists, as he does here, that this correction is already written into Lacan, whose "capture" of the Imaginary by the Symbolic "rather perfectly repeats the formal as well as the thematic logic of Shakespeare's [and the dark lady's] 'perjur'd eye'" (45). Like Lacan's difference from Shakespeare, deconstruction's difference from Lacan is already an image of the difference in Lacan between the Symbolic and the Imaginary, as if deconstruction could only find its reflection in Lacan's "mirror stage."

What Fineman ultimately suggests is that contemporary theory finds in Shakespeare not a confirmation of its methods but an unsettling, because too perfect, repetition. In *Shakespeare's Perjured Eye* he considers two disjunctures of vision and language, the Shakespearean and the psychoanalytic, that finally cannot be distinguished when each becomes, internally and with respect to one other, the scene of this same disjuncture. Hence the reversible poles of "perhaps the question is by now familiar: Is Shakespeare Freudian or is Freud Shakespearean?" (46). In Freud's one essay devoted to Shakespeare, "The Theme of the Three Caskets," the caskets ultimately figure the three fates, but, for whatever reasons, Freud mentions nowhere that Shakespeare makes the same implicit connection in young Launcelot Gobbo's "Talk not of master Launcelot, father, for the young gentleman, according to Fates and Destinies, and such odd sayings, the Sisters Three, and such branches of learning, is indeed deceased, or as you would say in plain terms, gone to heaven" (2.2.60–65).[7] That Shakespeare and Shakespearean criticism might be indistinguishable ("hearing the Shakespearean echoes coalesce into [Freudian] science, it is difficult to determine who is accounting for whom"), or that the blurring of the distinction might actually be the goal of the latter, would be a pressing question only if one were concerned with reinvesting criticism itself with the pathos of the Shakespearean subject. It is with this question in mind, the question of the lyric voice in contemporary theory, that one would have to read all the autothematizations written into Fineman's book, all the deliberate attempts to displace or work through the difference between criticism and its object—the frequent "I will" constructions of the book's introduction and elsewhere; the first chapter's opening on "The sonnet begins"; the echoing grafts of criticism and text in sentences like "a disjunction occasioned by verbal duplicity, as when 'When my love swears that she is made of truth'" (17), "the withdrawn ambiguity of its explanatory 'since'— 'Since all alike my songs and praises be'—since this concessive particle . . ." (141), "'How like a winter hath my absence been' (97), and yet, 'And yet this time remov'd was summer's time'" (235); the literally self-conscious insertions of the first-person pronoun in sentences like

"It is not only because so many Renaissance sonnets in fact play upon this I-me-thou-thee conceit . . . that I . . ." (7), "I have characterized as the poet's doubly divided panegyric 'I' . . ." (220), "I am concerned with the place of this difference *within* the commonplace of reflexive reflection" (248); the ambiguous antecedent of *my* in "In Shakespeare's sonnets, I argue, the poet 'give[s] the lie to my true sight'" (15); the chiastic "this, I want to argue, is how it *feels* to be the subject of chiasmus" (241); the formal irony of "I have already mentioned, for example, the 're-turning' way in which . . ." (189), "I spoke earlier of the poet's sense of literary retrospection . . ." (262), "I cite this at such length because it is important to have a feel for the rhetorical excess that is characteristic of praise paradox . . ." (30); and so on. In each case such literary-critical displacements amount to little more than extended glosses on the pun written into the deflected specularity of *Shakespeare's Perjured I,* a homonym underlined in "I say a progress from eye to tongue" (170) and elsewhere. The reverse, the presence of the critical in the lyric voice, would be the pun on *essayed* in "Shakespeare's sonnets are written as though by a poet who has already essayed the paradox of praise" (29).

3

Among recent theorists of the theater Herbert Blau, Johannes Birringer, and Ned Lukacher have perhaps most consistently underscored this haunting of postwar criticism and theory by Shakespeare. According to Blau, "when the theatricalism of the sixties subsided in political life, one of the subtler things that happened to it, another form of going underground, was that it was—in the human sciences, philosophy, and literature—recycled or (re)sublimated *as theory*."[8] Birringer similarly remarks "the pervasive interpretive efforts with which the theoretical disciplines (literary theory, psychoanalysis, anthropology, semiology, philosophy, sociology, and so forth) approached their own epistemological searches and introspections in terms of the 'model of theater,' or the 'phantom of theater' as Roland Barthes called it, remembering Francis Bacon" (42). As Birringer observes of both Blau's *Take Up the Bodies* and his *Bloodied Thought,* "like [Hamlet's] Ghost these writings cross back and forth between theory and theater, conceptualization and act, mind and body, form and content, past and present, as if there was no crossing, no clear boundary" (90–91). In *Take Up the Bodies,* whose title takes up the closing speech of *Ham-*

let, "the central chapters . . . ('Origin of the Species,' 'Missing Persons,' 'Ghosting') . . . 'follow' the Ghost in Shakespeare's most famous play in ever-widening circles of abstraction."[9]

The importance of *Hamlet* to this proposed "release" of "Shakespeare's Will," as Fineman presents it, also figures prominently in two books by Lukacher, *Primal Scenes: Literature, Philosophy, Psychoanalysis* (1986) and *Daemonic Figures: Shakespeare and the Question of Conscience* (1994). In *Primal Scenes* "it is in 'The Murder of Gonzago' that we can see the emergence of a new and abyssal form of subjectivity," a subjectivity that returns to writers as diverse as Hegel, Nietzsche, Joyce, Goethe, Coleridge, and Eliot (208), the first of whom speculates near the close of his *Lectures on the History of Philosophy:*

> It goes ever on and on, because spirit is progress alone. Spirit often seems to have forgotten and lost itself, but inwardly opposed to itself, it is inwardly working ever forward as Hamlet says of the ghost of his father, "Well done, old mole"— until grown enough in itself it bursts asunder the crust of earth which divided it from its sun, its Notion, so that the earth crumbles away.[10]

In *Daemonic Figures* Lukacher still more compellingly draws the history of philosophy into "the site whence the daemon calls" while proposing that the philosophic history of conscience from Plato to Heidegger culminates in Shakespeare, in a theory demonically turned theater within which Heidegger's "readiness" (*Bereitschaft*) recasts Hamlet's "the readiness is all" and the philosopher's very "silence" on Shakespeare "belies the profound affinity between his thinking (*Denken*) and Shakespeare's poetic saying (*Sage*) of the words for being."[11] For within "the presencing power of language" (18)—"the daemon is a figure for the god that dwells in language" (7)—"poetry itself has been transformed by the event of Shakespeare's signature and by the force of a linguistic will" (124 n. 47). Here Lukacher's reading dovetails with Fineman's, for, as Lukacher himself observes, "Fineman's reading of the sonnets reveals Shakespeare as the last god, the one who dares to dwell near the unfathomable lack in Being." Thus, for Lukacher "it is in this daemonic place that Shakespeare discerns the bond between the poet and friend whom he, in effect, carries within himself and who, as Fineman remarks, 'thereby divides the poet from himself'" (119). For in this case Shakespeare's dividing "friend," if only syntactically, is Fineman himself: "and who, as Fineman remarks, 'thereby divides.'" The theory, in turn, and not simply the theater, is once again autobiographical, and literal, like the "*cl-*" in *Luk*acher's account of *cleave, cling, clamour,* and *close* in *Macbeth:* "the *cl-* is distinct from all these semantic elements. It calls on Shakespeare from another depth of language. Duncan is 'clear in his office'" (191–92). So Lukacher's *Daemonic Figures,* taking up the very Shakespearean burrowing, and borrowing, to which it refers in *Hamlet,* refigures the play's "abyssal subjectivity" in theory but also, as for Freud, Fineman, Greenblatt, Rogin, and Wilde, in name: "This is one Lucianus, nephew to the king. . . . 'A poisons him i' th' garden for his estate. His name's Gonzago; the story is extant, and written in very choice Italian" (3.2.244–63).

Hamlet thus "haunts" the development of psychoanalysis in Freud but also from Freud to Lacan, who very much plays mad-feigning son to the mourning memory of a ghost-father Freud in his seminal essay "Desire and the Interpretation of Desire in *Hamlet*":

> What gives the phallus its particular value? Freud replies, as always, without the slightest precaution—he bowls us over, and thank God he did it till the day he died, for otherwise he never could have finished what he still had to lay out [*tracer*] in his field of work—Freud replies that it's a narcissistic demand [*exigence*] made by the subject.[12]

Lacan's "he bowls us over, and thank God he did it till the day he died" shifts, in a moment of literal psychoanalytic transference, Hamlet's narcissistic incorporation of his ghostly father onto Lacan's own remembrance of an almost supernatural Freud. Beginning, then, with the essay's title, "Desire and the Interpretation of Desire," Lacan's revision of Freud is everywhere a revival, desire *and* the interpretation of desire. In the essay that directly follows Lacan's in the anthology *Literature and Psychoanalysis,* Daniel Sibony's "*Hamlet:* A Writing Effect," Freudian psychoanalysis represents one more "writing effect" of Shakespeare's most psychologically demanding tragedies, but so, within just this filial succession, do the "writings" of Lacan:

> Freud, in a learned footnote in his *Interpretation of Dreams,* walks right into the middle of this plot, this fratricide, as if the murder of Gonzago, which took place in Vienna (and the text of which is after all the nucleus of the play), . . . were plunged

into the future and there received its echo, emanating from another dead father, Freud's father Jakob. . . . Or Lacan: who has continued this writing in the graph of its desire and could equally well attempt to chain up the beast again with his knots.[13]

Within the father-son dialectic set out by Jakob, Freud, and Jacques, Freud enacts his own oedipal theory with filial respect not simply to but also for Shakespeare, even as, at one Joycean remove, Lacan's paradoxical *Ecrits*, as Jean-Luc Nancy and Philippe Lacoue-Labarthe observe, "draws from the occasion of a 'discourse' in the oratory sense, that is, from a single grasp, a direct (if not simple), immediate, and for that reason sensible apprehension offered to a university audience before being offered in the *Ecrits*, which is, one should not forget, 'a title more ironic than one might think.'"[14] Hence, in the *Hamlet* Seminar, Lacan's quasi-theatrical "Let me ask you to return to the graveyard scene, to which I have already referred you three times" (35). Even "winding up," Lacan's identification with Hamlet, and therefore with Laertes, is all-consuming:

> The third stage, to which I have already directed your attention several times, is the graveyard scene, in the course of which Hamlet is finally presented with the possibility of winding things up, of rushing to his fate. . . .
> I should be able to finish up next time. (23–24)

The Seminar thus ends in the only manner it can, by literally turning into *Hamlet* through a disappearing act that makes Lacan, in the final analysis, the subject of the action par excellence:

> "The body is with the king"—he doesn't use the word corpse, please notice—"but the king is not with the body." Replace the word "king" with the word "phallus," and you'll see that that's exactly the point—the body is bound up [*engagé*] in this matter of the phallus—and how—but the phallus, on the contrary, is bound to nothing: it always slips through our fingers.

> *Hamlet:* The king is a thing —
> *Guildenstern:* A thing, my lord?
> *Hamlet:* Of nothing.
>
> (29 April 1959) (52–53)

4

The history of philosophy (and therefore of the academy) thus haunts *Hamlet*, but Hamlet's Wittenberg, again, already haunts philosophy by ruling in everything Socrates rules out—"that greatest of all falsehoods on great subjects, which the misguided poet told about Ouranos." For the violence at the center of the play also undermines the difference between the language of the university and that of the theater ("My lord, you played once in the university, you say?" [3.2.98–99]), transforming the theater itself into a university now refigured as the site of the archetypal historical violence that never stops haunting the *play* ("I did enact Julius Caesar. I was killed i' th' Capitol; Brutus killed me" [103–4]):

> *Hamlet:* But what, in faith, make you from Wittenberg . . . ?
> *Horatio:* My lord, I came to see your father's funeral.
> *Hamlet:* I prithee do not mock me, fellow student.
>   I think it was to see my mother's wedding.
>
> (1.2.168–78)

The action returns to the academy ("fellow studient"), but now the *matter* is the mother ("but to the matter: my mother, you say" [3.2.324–25]) and the father the *further* ("were she ten times our mother. Have you any further trade with us?" [333–34]) that carries the action beyond even Hamlet's "There are more things in heaven and earth, Horatio, / Than are dreamt of in your philosophy" (1.5.166–67):

> Remember thee!
> Yea, from the table of my memory
> I'll wipe away all trivial fond records,
> All saws of books, all forms, all pressures past
> That youth and observation copied there,
> And thy commandment all alone shall live
> Within the book and volume of my brain,
> Unmixed with baser matter.
>
> (1.5.97–104)[15]

The Ghost of Hamlet thus haunts philosophy not just after but *in* the play, which ultimately delimits the language of the university by recasting it, with everything Socrates rules out *in rule,* as theater.

Within the same theater-theory continuum, only in reverse, Sandra M. Gilbert and Susan Gubar's essay "Masterpiece Theatre: An
Academic Melodrama" literally recasts the institutional debate over
literary criticism and theory as a play, and one centered on an
unidentified manuscript whose identity proves equally Shakespearean. Thus, "in a sailboat off the coast of Southern California
[Lacuna Breach?]," J. Hillis Miller and Harold Bloom wonder what
unknown assailant has perilously tied—the plot of "An Academic
Melodrama"—which unknown text to "the fast track," prompting
Miller's "To go or not to go! A good example of metaphysical undecidability."[16] An hour before, in Washington, D.C., education secretary
William Bennett and National Endowment for the Humanities director Lynne Cheney share fears that the unknown text "might be by Milton or Shakespeare. It might speak 'to the deepest concerns we all
have as human beings.' . . . The ideologues, the theorists—they're to
blame" (698). On a small commuter plane en route to Boondock State
(the scene of the crime) E. D. Hirsch Jr. corners a basketball player
returning home from a recruiting visit:

> "*Romeo and Juliet.* A TRAGEDY by William SHAKESPEARE about
> two 'STAR-CROSSED LOVERS' whose passionate love for each
> other ends in death because of the senseless feud between
> their families. The line 'ROMEO, ROMEO! WHEREFORE ART THOU
> ROMEO?' is well known." [*He chomps a peanut*]. (708)

In each case the unknown text is literally Shakespearean, as if that
text (and even, in "WHEREFORE ART THOU ROMEO," that feud) engendered
the debate. Thus, in the small commuter plane carrying E. D. Hirsch
Jr. and his would-be basketball charge to the scene of the crime, S. G.
(Sandra Gilbert and Susan Gubar—but also, in this context, Stephen
Greenblatt, and even, across this same gendered difference, Susan
Grindstone)—asks of the unknown text: "What if it's a female-
authored text? It might have been stolen from the *Norton Anthology
of Literature by Women*" (707). For at stake in this debate, as in Martin's trial, is the difference between the theater and the theory, sexual
difference, that each rigorously "unsexes," even as Hamlet's "Now,
mother, what's the matter?" (3.4.7) resonates from the same theoreti-
cal-theatrical matrix as Gertrude's absolutely central—what Freud
would call the dream's "navel"—"More *matter* with less art" (2.2.95).
"'Ho, ho, ho!' he (or maybe she) adds," as the mysterious tome is knot-
ted fast to the fast track (695).

Within the new historicism, in this regard, Fineman's more properly Barberian assimilation of Shakespeare, psychoanalysis, and cultural anthropology deepens the ultimately institutional refashioning of theater by theory in the new historicism by way of the same "above all" subject, Hamlet—more *Martin*, Gertrude might have said, with less Arnaud. For like Martin and Arnaud, or psychoanalysis and Renaissance culture, their own critical difference is a function of the same archetypal drama, and this is perhaps why Greenblatt, on the first page of his introduction to *Shakespeare's Will*, writes of Fineman's own reliance on the figure of "cross-coupling" with reference to just this play:

> Fineman was a wonderfully gifted constructor of chiastic structures—what he would call (with a nod to Elizabethan rhetoric) "cross-coupled" relationships—and much of his writing through his career took the form of a charting of these structures in individual plays or poems. Because Hamlet—to give a single example of this charting from "Fratricide and Cuckoldry"—"is his own Jaques, just as he is his own Orlando, it therefore makes more sense that the heartsick, melancholy skepticism of the hero is built not only into his own end but into the end of his world. But so too, at the end, Hamlet, like Jaques, is sent to a sacred resting place where for all his heroism he can do no further harm." (*SW*, ix–x)

Here, from the play to its reception, the example instances a larger cross-coupling of the drama under discussion—"Hamlet, like Jaques, is sent to a sacred resting place"—and the ongoing discussion itself. The same subtext returns with much greater directness, and with still more manifest attention to the problematic limits of the "subject," at the close of Greenblatt's introduction:

> He must have felt in the end that his body had violated the dream of his writing, the dream that there is nothing *but* writing. And yet perhaps that is only *my* projection, my sense of violation and loss; he behaved through it all as if his body, even in its excruciating self-betrayal and vanishing, were somehow fulfilling the dream. Sitting by his bed, I said, in the feeble attempt at consolation to which one is driven in such situations, that he was just going a little before the rest of us.

> "O worthy pioneer," he replied with a smile, wittily playing
> half-adoring, half-mocking Hamlet to his own grave-digging
> Ghost. He told me something else. He couldn't eat any
> longer—that part of his bodily life was already over—for he
> couldn't swallow. But he said that he was getting incredible
> pleasure from taking sips of New York Seltzer and letting the
> bubbles burst on his lips and tongue. (*SW*, xix)

Drawing out this almost Horatian tableau ("the rest of us" / "the rest
is silence"—"O worthy pioneer"), Greenblatt's introduction to *Shakespeare's Will* ends by turning into, and out of, *Hamlet* ("to tell my
story" / "he told me something else").

Just before this final evocation of the Ghost's overarching
"Remember me" (1.5.91), Greenblatt refers to Fineman's essay on the
new historicism, "The History of the Anecdote: Fiction and Fiction,"
as "his last essay" (*SW*, xix). Nevertheless, and for reasons that will be
explained in a moment, footnotes in the subsequent text make clear
that "Fiction and Fiction" "was originally delivered as a talk at a conference on 'The New Historicism: The Boundaries of Social Science'
at the West Coast Humanities Institute, Stanford University, Oct. 9,
1987" (*SW*, 76), while the essay "Shakespeare's Ear," published
posthumously in a special issue of the journal *Representations* "in
memory of Joel Fineman" and included as the last chapter of *Shakespeare's Will*, was "read to the Shakespeare Association of America,
Boston, Massachusetts, April 30, 1988" (*SW*, 231). In the issue of *Representations* in which "Shakespeare's Ear" first appeared, the lastness
of this particular essay further characterizes Leo Lowenthal's memo-
rable account of its completion, or incompletion (to which Greenblatt alludes in his reference to "Fiction and Fiction" as Fineman's
last essay):

> A week or ten days before Joel died, a day after he had returned
> to his house from the hospital, he requested that his Macin-
> tosh computer, mounted by his bedside by his nephew, be
> turned on: with feeble fingers and utmost concentration, try-
> ing to fend off the effects of morphine, he managed to recall
> his essay on "Shakespeare's Ear," which was to be incorpo-
> rated in his new book and which he had been hoping to finish
> before the end. The image of his emaciated, dying body com-
> pelled by the creative mind to detain, for a moment, its inex-
> orable devastation is lodged in my memory as a paradigm of
> immortality.

On occasion Joel permitted himself the utterance "It is not fair." I am standing here before you more than twice his age—and have to say: indeed, it is not fair.[17]

Here, as in Greenblatt's introduction to *Shakespeare's Will*, a slightly less explicit *Hamlet* backdrop—the nephew, the debilitating effects of morphine and the poisoned rapier coursing through Hamlet, the post-Fall violence of firstborn Cain turned bedside "Macintosh," Hamlet's own "Are you fair?" (*Perjured Eye*, 130)—occasions a similar displacement from the central drama in Fineman's writing to that writing itself. Giving point to the motivating pun in Shakespeare's last name while underscoring just this literary-critical displacement (the importance, again, of being Ear-nest), "Shakespeare's Ear" concludes with a discussion of Derridean "otobiography":

> The metaphoremes, and the erotics that inform them, that appear in Derrida's text do not come from nowhere; quite the contrary, I propose that they come from the Renaissance in general, and from Shakespeare in particular. To show that, however, it would be necessary to show that for Shakespeare it is specifically the ear that is the organ of the text, of the specifically typographic text, and that is something, given the constraints of time, as well as the nature of things, that must, for now, be postponed, though Shakespeare's sonnet 46 would be one place to begin. (231)

To this closing gesture, which also marks a beginning, Fineman attaches the following note:

> Remember the "question" of the text—cf. Dora, Lacan, the moon and the semicolon—i.e., the rhetorical question. People don't want to read nowadays; they substitute thematic reaction for reading. The force of the story is to show that textuality predicates a specific sexuality and ideology, and that if people aren't willing to read, they will be caught up in this fetishistic project.

This is how the note reads, and the essay ends, in the memorial issue of *Representations* in which it first appeared; in the version of "Shakespeare's Ear" published in *Shakespeare's Will*, and somewhat mysteriously, since the *Representations* essay is already posthumous and cited as the source for the version in *Shakespeare's Will,* the note (and the book) ends:

> —remember the "question" of the text, cf. Dora, Lacan, the moon and the semicolon; the rhetorical question
>
> —people don't want to read nowadays, substituting thematic reaction for reading
>
> —force of the story is to show that textuality predicates a specific sexuality and ideology, and if people aren't willing to read, they will be caught up in this fetishistic project.

The Place of the University:
Shakespeare and Multiculturalism

In the following remarks on the state and the university in Shake-spearean studies and postwar criticism, this chapter explores the recent institutional emphasis on ethnic and cultural studies in the work of recognizably leftist academics, but does so from the left, argu-ing that such critical emphases are no more demystified or ideologi-cally subversive than the more traditional work from which they dis-sent. In so arguing, I want to gesture toward two interrelated readings of multiculturalism, both of which I will proceed to qualify in some-what substantive ways. My first thesis is that present-day literary crit-icism and theory function in the postwar, postmodern university in precisely the way that Shakespearean drama has sometimes been understood to function in the early modern national theater—namely, as the site of an institutionalized subversion that actually strengthens the very centralizing authority it ostensibly opposes. Hence, as David Rieff and others have suggested, the somewhat sudden institutional rise of multiculturalism at a time—the 1980s—of an unprecedented swing to the right in domestic and foreign affairs, culminating, at both extremes, around the time of the Gulf War (the notorious "Thought Police on Campus" issue of *Newsweek* magazine asks across the top of the same cover: "Containing Saddam: Can Diplomacy Do the Job?").[1] My second thesis, following from this first, is that the relation of the new left to the far right is not one of contradiction but is, in fact, a continuum. The people who brought us Willy Horton brought us Clarence Thomas. And Saddam Hussein, the black rapist raping Kuwait. Who are these people, and how can they be stopped? More important, can they be stopped?

Let me begin with the second thesis first, since it is so conve-niently summarized by the gentleman referred to a moment ago, David Rieff, in an August 1993 article in *Harper's* magazine entitled "Multiculturalism's Silent Partner: It's the Newly Globalized Consumer Economy, Stupid." The title says it all. "Are the multicultural-ists," Rieff asks, "truly unaware of how closely their treasured catch-phrases—'cultural diversity,' 'difference,' the need to 'do away with boundaries'—resemble the stock phrases of the modern corporation: 'product diversification,' 'the global marketplace,' and 'the boundary-less company'?" (66). According to Rieff, "if any group has embraced the rallying cry 'Hey, hey, ho, ho, Western culture's got to go,' it is the world business elite" (68)—the multicultural university, inside out, as multinational corporation. The dialectic here is almost Adornian, even Kierkegaardian, and from it derives the multicultural assault on artistic merit as antidemocratic, "for if all art is deemed as good as all other art, and, for that matter, if the point of art is not greatness but the production of works of art that reflect the culture and aspirations of various ethnic, sexual, or racial subgroups within a society, then one is in a position to increase supply almost at will in order to meet increases in demand" (64). This seamless extension of the economic into the academic also explains "the readiness of administrators of Ivy League colleges to accept what is, by any standard, a sweeping over-haul of history, philosophy, and literature curricula," for "why should it matter to the provost if his professional advisers think the institu-tion should start recruiting Chicano-studies experts and let Chauceri-ans gradually go out of stock? People make decisions like this in cor-porate America every day; indeed, these are the decisions CEOs are paid to make" (63–64).

Multiculturalism, read multiculturally, is thus itself an effect, an epiphenomenal consequence, of the same commodifying and homoge-nizing forces that it sets out to demystify. Within the academy this left-right combination (the metaphor is from boxing) entails no con-tradiction because the impelling force behind it is economic, *pre*-ideo-logical, which in turn is what makes the contradiction so "interdisci-plinary"—the Marxists with their swimming pools; the civil libertarians with their water buffalo; the multiculturalists with their Ph.D.'s in English and a minor in American Studies; the reformists with their packed search committees; the deconstructionists with their chairmanships; the African Americanists with their bathrooms (and he a fine and talented scholar); the radical feminists with their graduate student belles (and some the same); the aspiring graduate stu-dents with their robotic sloganeering; the traditionalists, finally, with all this, all this—irony is too charitable, and self-righteous hypocrisy, alas, is not blunt enough.

And yet such double standards, common as they are, render valu-able glimpses at the all but invisible point of the circle around which the whole enterprise may be said to turn. For where economy leads, Marx showed, ideology will follow, in this case to the same left-right continuum. To cite only one particularly egregious example, in a wide-ranging and politically alert account of recent literary criticism entitled *After Bakhtin* (1990), David Lodge cites with evident approval Edward Said's assertion that "it is no accident that the emergence of so narrowly defined a philosophy of pure textuality and critical non-interference [as deconstruction] has coincided with the ascendancy of Reaganism—or for that matter with a new cold war, increased militarism and defense spending, and a massive turn to the right in matters touching the economy, social services, and organized labor"; yet the frontispiece to Lodge's *After Bakhtin* boldly proclaims: "If the 1960s was the decade of structuralism, and the 1970s the decade of deconstruction, then the 1980s have been dominated by the discovery and dissemination of Mikhail Bakhtin's work."[2] Much more generally, feminist criticism staunchly opposes the hyperpatriarchal agenda embodied by Freud's oedipal model of desire, but the movement's own desire—namely, to do away with, bypass, deconstruct, or rewrite the father in order to possess, or repossess, the mother—is Freud's oedipal scenario in something like its purest institutional form.

Ideology critique, too, is not the most but the least neutral of all critical paradigms. "The accusation of being in ideology," Louis Althusser warns, "only applies to others, never to oneself."[3] Many years earlier the great cultural theorist Karl Mannheim drew attention to the same contradiction in *Ideology and Utopia* (1936): "It might have been expected that long ago Marxism would have formulated in a theoretical way the fundamental findings . . . concerning the relationship between human thought and the conditions of existence *in general*," adding that mystification "was perceived only in the thought of the opponent."[4] And so, it would seem, is it perceived today, left and right: "the accusation of being in ideology only applies to others, never to oneself." Yet, in its own theoretical terms, campus radicalism, like 1990s conservatism, necessarily derives from a far more contradictory and even subordinate relation to the state on the part of the university, and above all on the part of literary studies. For on two coordinated fronts, the economic and the ideological, the opposition of left and right in the postmodern academy is not so much diametrical as dialectical—that is to say, historical, even "contemporary." There is a contradiction, but only because that contradiction covers over a still deeper, and much more anonymous, continuum.

Which brings us back around, finally, to our first thesis, that multiculturalism functions in the present-day, postmodern university exactly like the literature, and above all the theater, it studies—institutionally, ideologically, and conceptually. On the one hand, Shakespeare himself very much represents both the great white *Will* of a violently patriarchal canon, the *barred*, and the strong precursor poet, the great white *Male*, for many of multiculturalism's most influential authors and critics, from Virginia Woolf to Maya Angelou. One striking instance of this approach-avoidance relation to Shakespeare on the part of multiculturalism is provided by Richard Levin's essay "Feminist Thematics and Shakespearean Tragedy," published in *PMLA* (March 1988). The essay, pronouncing feminist criticism of Shakespeare "reductive," prompted a defiant letter of protest signed by twenty-four correspondents pronouncing Levin's own essay "reductive." The controversy is therefore Shakespearean not just because Shakespeare occasions it but because Levin's essay on feminism and Shakespearean tragedy resembles nothing so nearly as *King Lear*, unrolling its own critical map in order to discover, as the king announces, which of his daughters "shall we say doth love us most" (1.1.51). Echoing Lear at the opening of the play, "today," Levin writes in his opening paragraph, feminist criticism of Shakespeare "may surely be said to have come of age and to have taken its place as one of the established branches of Shakespearean research."[5] In a series of pregnant metaphors the same paragraph strikingly records the "remarkable growth" of feminist criticism in the "brief period" since the publication of Juliet Dusinberre's *Shakespeare and the Nature of Women* in 1975, concluding that such criticism "has produced a substantial body of publications" (125). The spirited letter of protest that greeted Levin's article, then, would be the same play several acts later ("accusing us of his own flaws, Levin paternally tries to preempt our strengths by recommending our project to us as if it were his idea").[6] Levin's essay, in turn, is "tired, muddled, unsophisticated" (77–78). From "feminist thematics" to "Shakespearean tragedy," the controversy surrounding Levin's essay is thus not simply thematically but formally "Shakespearean."

So, to cite one more example, is Gerald Graff's equally representative "Beyond the Culture Wars," in which the immediate object of debate between an "Older Male Professor" (OMP) and a "Young Feminist Professor" (YFP) is Matthew Arnold's "Dover Beach," but whose dialogue again quickly segues into Shakespeare:

> OMP *(furiously stirring his Coffee-mate):* In *my* humble opinion—reactionary though I suppose it is now—"Dover Beach" is one of the great masterpieces of the Western

tradition, a work that, until recently, at least, every seriously educated person took for granted as part of the cultural heritage.

YFP: Perhaps, but is that altogether to the credit of the cultural heritage? Take those lines addressed to the woman: "Ah, love, let us be true to one another . . ." and so forth. In other words, protect and console me, my dear—as it's the function of your naturally more spirited sex to do. . . . We *should* teach "Dover Beach." We should teach it as an example of the phallocentric discourse that it is.

OMP: That's the trouble with you people; you seem to treat "Dover Beach" as if it were a piece of political propaganda rather than a work of art. . . . "Dover Beach" is no more about gender politics than *Macbeth* is about the Stuart monarchical succession.

YFP: But *Macbeth is* about the Stuart monarchical succession, among other things—or at least its original audience may well have thought so. It's about gender politics, too. Why does Lady Macbeth have to "unsex" herself to qualify to commit murder? . . . What you take to be the universal human experience in Arnold and Shakespeare is male experience presented as if it were universal.[7]

Like Levin's "Feminist Thematics and Shakespearean Tragedy," or even Gilbert and Gubar's "Masterpiece Theatre: An Academic Melodrama," the debate not only carries over into Shakespeare but displaces the properly oedipal drama of the play under discussion—"furiously stirring his Coffee-*mate*," the sudden question of "Stuart monarchical succession," the overall struggle and fight of "Older Male" and "Young Feminist"—onto the debate itself. In the process the institutional force of Graff's presumably activist determination to "teach the conflicts" assumes its own conventional thematics and form, from the debate over "Dover Beach" to its almost medieval *conflictus* of male tradition and female change.

Institutionally, then, there are important literary and theatrical dimensions to a Rieff-like conception of the postmodern academy as late capitalist "department" store, or of the early modern theater as protocapitalist "dream" factory. For like the ideological field subtending postwar academia and the nation-state, the one characterizing the early modern stage in Shakespeare's day situates a still more radically performative national theater within a still more absolutist monarchy while negotiating the movements, theorems, and controversies of aristocratic rebels, Aristotelean republicans, theosophic monarchists, skeptical humanists, parliamentary pluralists, common law libertarians, reactionary Puritans, free-thinking anarchists, and so on. Otherness, in turn, is the same in Shakespeare and multiculturalism because, at either institutional extreme, when an irreducible difference to self can no longer be controlled as such the *result* is racism (Iago's "I am not what I am" [1.1.65]) or sexism (Richard III's "What do I fear? Myself?" [5.3.182]) or anti-Semitism (Antonio's "In sooth, I know not why I am so sad" [*Merchant of Venice*, 1.1.1]. So multiculturalism seeks to dramatize and expose the more contemporary persistence of such self-repression in someone like erstwhile presidential hopeful and former Ku Klux Klan leader David Duke, who is also the author of two books, a phony handbook for black revolutionaries published under the name Mohammed X and a fake sex manual for women by one Dorothy Vanderbilt. In each case, when an irreducible difference to self can no longer be controlled as such—Mohammed, Malcolm X, the Vanderbilt of Duke's deep-south alma mater Louisiana State University turned feminized scene of writing (Vander-*built*), the Dorothy of Kansas and Toto but also of Duke's own Oz-like pretensions to "Grand Wizard"—the result is racism or sexism or anti-Semitism (the other, again, "Dorothy," as author). Multiculturalism is thus Shakespearean not only because intolerance for each is the *repression* of self-difference, but because in multiculturalism the irreducible difference to self that is no longer controllable as such is, institutionally, the theater.

Thus, while Shakespeare himself is significantly and even necessarily "shorn" of his universality in the work of many writers and critics associated with multiculturalism, this demystification of Shakespeare's cultural transcendence need not lead to what Peter Erickson has called an "oversimplified version of Shakespearean/minority tension," which assumes "that, since Shakespeare is a fixed, unchanging point, then all change can be portrayed as challenges from without."[8] On the contrary, Erickson argues in *Rewriting Shakespeare, Rewriting Ourselves*,

> this image of Shakespeare neglects or denies the reformulation of the canon from inside through the reinterpretation of canonical figures, including Shakespeare. Within current Shakespeare studies, new historicists and feminist critics agree that Shakespeare's work cannot be treated as aesthetically autonomous or historically contingent. Like a protective

mantle shorn of its magical efficacy, the assertion of Shakespeare's special universality, which seemed hitherto to
exempt his works from critical questions concerning gender,
class, and race, and national identity, no longer convinces. The
result is a complicated reassessment of Shakespeare that con-
tributes to the larger project of rewriting the Renaissance and
of reevaluating the entire literary tradition. (5)

Like the Shakespeare of Graff's Young Female Professor ("what you
take to be the universal human experience in Arnold and Shakespeare
. . . is male experience presented as if it were universal"), only posi-
tively, the Shakespeare of multiculturalism represents the most "aes-
thetically autonomous" of all authors and artists because, paradoxically, the most "historically contingent."

To cite only one brief example, Shakespeare's sonnet 107 claims to
transcend all history and chance because it is written, again, "with the
drops of this most balmy time":

Not mine own fears nor the prophetic soul
Of the wide world dreaming on things to come
Can yet the lease of my true love control,
Supposed as forfeit to a confined doom.
The mortal moon hath her eclipsed endured,
And the sad augurs mock their own presage,
Incertainties now crown themselves assured,
And peace proclaims olives of endless age.
Now with the drops of this most balmy time
My love looks fresh, and Death to me subscribes,
Since spite of him I'll live in this poor rhyme,
While he insults o'er dull and speechless tribes.
    And thou in this shalt find thy monument,
    When tyrants' crests and tombs of brass are spent.

In *mortal moon* and *crown* the second stanza contains the only direct
reference to Elizabeth in the sonnets, and according to the following
relation: as the queen rules all space, so the poet rules all time. In
"peace proclaims olives of endless age" the two desires further converge in a pun on "I'll live" from line 11—"And peace proclaims *I'll
lives* of endless age."[9] Superimposing, in turn, one imperial desire over
the other, the poem announces its own triumph over yet unborn "dull
and speechless tribes." The poem's "balmy time," too, further con-
notes the new world tropics of these same "wide world" energies,

making the object of desire ("*My love* looks fresh") the subject ("can yet the lease of *my true love* control"). The sonnet thus models and finally builds its own temporal imperialism on the spatial imperialism of the crown, but the more universal or timeless this makes the poetry, the more local and contingent it becomes.

Such, then, runs the double thesis with which we began. On the one hand, the university functions, like the theater, as a site of institutionalized subversion, waxing increasingly militant in accordance with an ever more influential conservatism. At the same time (thesis 2), this dialectic of subversion and containment itself derives from larger, more impersonal economic and institutional practices within which that contradiction dissolves, yielding, again, the many glaring inconsistencies between the theory and the practice of "multiculturalism." As Kant observed almost two hundred years ago in his brief treatise on the changing German university, "Der Streit der Fakultäten" (The Conflict of the Faculties):

> The class of the higher faculties (in a manner of speaking the right wing of the parliament of knowledge) defends the statutes of the government; however, in a free constitution, as any which respects the truth must be, there must also exist an opposition audience (the left), for without the severe scrutiny and objections of the latter, the government would not be sufficiently informed of what can be helpful or harmful to it.[10]

Some two centuries hence, the various rightist epithets attached to leftist multiculturalism by the popular media—McCarthyism, puritanism, newspeak, apartheid, Stalinism, feminazism, Maoism, tribalism, and the like—signify from afar, in their very extremity, just this closed institutional circle of far right agendas and new left orthodoxies. All the while, administrators and academicians rush to embrace substantive reforms, seemingly mindless that their respective institutions and departments will be here, properly and very savvily managed, forever. And what, without waxing the least bit histrionic or hysterical, is the unspoken economic agenda driving all this institutional reform? The obsolescence of the university, which for so long drove the engines of the capitalist machine (hence, incidentally, the seemingly unrelated politically correct assaults on fraternities, athletic programs, standardized testing, endowments, student government, admissions, resident housing, free speech, dress codes, foreplay, mascots, and the like). Indeed, if such obsolescence were an unspoken goal, what three better developments than: (1) academicians fiercely devaluing the canonical works whose study separates the university from finishing schools; (2) radical leftist academics publicly breaking with the more moderate constituencies served by those bloated institutions; and (3) a fierce anti-intellectualism inside, and not simply outside, the halls of academe?

And yet, for all this, multiculturalism is also a powerfully co-optive version, as Sacvan Bercovitch underscores, of an old-fashioned democratic consensus whose "patchwork quilt" vision of America "is the reverse side of the familiar stars and stripes; multi-culturalism is the hyphenated America writ large."[11] In *Seductive Reasoning: Pluralism as the Problematic of Contemporary Literary Theory* Ellen Rooney makes much the same point when she notes how "the very notion of pluralistic society is often identified with the United States as such, and, simultaneously, it is consistently associated with U.S. foreign policy."[12] But, while Bercovitch and Rooney are somewhat more optimistic about the prospects for multiculturalism than is Rieff, "the trap," Bercovitch writes,

> lies in the way that the challenge itself may become the means for avoiding the questions raised by dissensus. Every ideology construes its own way into this trap. The American way is to turn potential conflict into a quarrel about fusion and fragmentation. It is a fixed match, a debate with a foregone conclusion and a ready formula for reaching it: fusion *and* fragmentation, a continual oscillation between harmony-in-diversity and diversity-in-harmony. It is the hermeneutics of laissez-faire. All conflicts are obviated by the continual flow of the one into the many, and the many into the one, as in Adam Smith's theory of the general will. . . . (373)

The multicultural dialectic of subversion and containment, the one into the many and the many into the one, thus characterizes not only early modern drama in an absolutist state but also, almost two centuries later, that very drama's own institutionalized subversion in, and as, American "dissensus" (Bercovitch's "foregone conclusion" [*Othello*, 3.3.428]). As Montrose observes of the various polemics in "Professing the Renaissance," "whatever other responses they may provoke, such discourses provide confirmation that the university is perceived to be a site for the contestation as well as the reproduction of ideological dominants; that there is something immediately important at stake in our reading and teaching of Shakespeare; and that, if we suddenly discover ourselves to be not marginal but rather in positions of cultural and institutional power, we are also now compelled to choose if, when and how to employ that power" (29). As Jean Howard similarly remarks, "there being no real, no Edenic Shakespeare, it follows that in constructing him and his texts we lay bare, in part, our own politics and our own values, and that fact should not be hidden from our students and colleagues behind a stance of supposed objectivity. Moreover, it *matters* whose Shakespeare prevails."[13]

Affirmative action and its effects on the academy offer a convenient insight into the place of the university in late-twentieth-century American culture. Though in theory only a marginal admissions and hiring policy, its representative centrality to higher education can be gauged by the enormous upheaval in the University of California system following the mandated elimination of hiring and recruiting practices based solely on race or gender. Why? That is, why such turmoil, culminating in the resignation of the university chancellor?

Clearly, the university today has taken on a political significance that goes far beyond the teaching, say, of political science. The great fault lines of social organization—race, class, gender—surface there with all the force of their post-Marlovian counterparts in the Renaissance theater. The culture wars played out for mass (middle-class) consumption on the early modern stage return with double force to the postwar academy. Ideologically, in turn, the place of the postmodern university, like the plays of the early modern theater, simultaneously concentrates enormous historical and cultural energies in the service of an increasingly powerful state apparatus and seeks to subvert them, whether in the name of entertainment or instruction (a performative-constative distinction whose deconstruction is therefore at the center, or noncenter, of poststructuralist criticism and theory). The expanding circulation of capital and shifting class structures that underwrite the rise of the Renaissance popular theater increasingly govern and shape postwar academe, whose symbolic presence at the center of industry, the military, and power corresponds to that of the theater. Multiculturalism, then, completes this institutional displacement with something like its most general, or "wide world," manifestation, as Montrose and Howard affirm.

Today, in post-Reagan-Bush, post-Clinton America, multiculturalism is forever removed from its dialectical origins in 1980s conservatism—critical legal studies goes to Washington. Heterodoxically, however, the worst thing that could have happened to the multicultural movement was the election of a liberal Democrat as president, and after Bill Clinton's election it would seem safe to say that the movement continued to lose, rather than gain, a certain amount of momentum and direction. And so, paradoxically, will it continue to falter, even as its core values and assumptions come to appear increasingly orthodox. For in sharp contrast to either Reagan or Bush, whose administrations blazoned what they took to be the academic and artistic excesses of the left, Clinton's ideological aloofness from the closed circle of academic left and right may be measured by the degree to which, in twice seeking election, he symbolically shunned the far left of the Democratic Party, as if that constituency represented an obstacle, rather than a boost, to his bid for the presidency. With the gays in the military debacle he almost lost; the left almost beat him. It was a leak, they leaked. And so, in a bit of bold and astute political maneuvering, Reagan's senior advisor David Gergen temporarily stepped in as Clinton's, closing the ranks. PC, then, does not necessarily stand for President Clinton, and where it does—in the appointment, for example, of the insufferable Sheldon Hackney as heir-apparent to the NEH throne vacated by Lynne (or is it Lon?) Cheney—there is he most vulnerable. For truly, can anyone really vote for a man who attends a dinner party at Sheldon Hackney's—that champion of the downtrodden's—summer home? Luckily for multiculturalism, its own institutional fortunes are by no means tied solely or even chiefly to post-Reagan-Bush, post-Clinton America—fortunes, again, that may have reached their ideological peak around the time of the Gulf War. "Cut it off and kill it," that was the order; bag *dad*, "the mother of all battles"—the battle of mimetic rivals, that is, of mimetic oil men, *over* mother. At the least, literary criticism can take some comfort in finding its own institutional hysterias replayed on the national, and international, stage, but that, I have tried to suggest, was inevitable.

Feminism and Theater
in *The Taming of the Shrew*

Whether Kate's final lord-of-creation moral in *The Taming of the Shrew* is tongue-in-cheek (the so-called revisionist school) or foot-in-mouth (the corresponding antirevisionist school) depends in part on the half-framed, and even half-tamed, nature of her story. For the play that Christopher Sly watches from the vantage of his unfinished Induction, *The Taming of the Shrew*, already represents a version, a gigantic "suppose," of the parallel play he acts both out and in, from Petruchio's triumphant "Come, Kate, we'll to bed" (5.2.184) and Sly's benighted "Madam, undress you, and come now to bed" (Ind.2.117) to the page boy's "My husband and my lord, my lord and husband" (Ind.2.106) and Kate's "Thy husband is thy lord, thy life, thy keeper" (5.2.146).[1] Whether such echoes add to the play's patriarchal merriment or undercut that moral is less clear, even if other such parallels are drawn—for example, Sly's "do I dream? Or have I dreamed till now" (Ind.2.69) and Kate "as one new risen from a dream" (4.1.186); the horses, hawks, hounds, hunt, help, horns, and herds bestowed on Sly (Ind.2.41–96) and the "carts" (1.1.55), "kites" (4.1.195), "cats" (2.1.278), "cates" (2.1.189), "cut" (4.3.121), "chat" (2.1.268), and "chattels" (3.2.230) to which Kate is compared (Gremio's "Our cake's dough" [1.1.108–9]); the debate over which of the three hounds, Silver, Belman, or Echo, is best (Ind.1.19–27) and the final wager over which of the three wives will come first, Bianca (Silver), the Widow (Belman), or Kate (Echo); the Lord's "I would not lose the dog for twenty pound" (Ind.1.21) and Petruchio's "Twenty crowns? / I'll venture so much of my hawk or hound" (5.2.71–72); the opening hunt generally and Tranio's "'Tis thought your deer does hold you at a bay" (5.2.26); Sly's acquaintance "Peter Turph" (Ind.2.94) and both Petruchio and his servant Peter; the Christ-bearer in "Christopher" ("score me up for the lyingest knave in Christendom" [Ind.2.24], "is not a comonty a Christmas gambold or a tumbling-trick" [138–39]) and the more elaborate conversion narrative of the larger taming story—

"Then God be blest, it is the blessèd sun" (4.5.18)—that carries the Christ-bearing Lucentio, Bianca, and Petruchio to "St. Luke's church" (4.4.88); the autobiographical subtext introduced by the actor in Shakespeare's own company Will Sly ("we came in with Richard Conqueror" [Ind.1.4–5]) and Petruchio's "will you, nill you, I will marry you" (2.1.271); and so on.[2] In each case, the play that Christopher Sly watches from the vantage of his unfinished Induction variously replays the story of his own Kate-like subjection by the Petruchio-like Lord, so that the moral is always less, and the lesson is always more, than meets the eye.

Whether, again, such echoes underscore or undermine the play's patriarchal merriment is further complicated because, however earnest the moral, the play already tells the story of its own Kate-like reception by the Petruchio-like spectator, recasting Petruchio's "taming-school" (4.2.54) as the taming, first, of "Xantippe" by "Socrates" (1.2.126) but also of "harmony" by "philosophy" (3.1.13–14), "Ovid" by "Aristotle" (1.1.32–33), "rhetoric" by "logic" (34–35), "music" by "mathematics" (36), "poesy" by "metaphysics" (37), "rhymes" by "Rheims" (2.1.80), and so on. From Sly's "by transmutation a bear-herd" (Ind.2.19–20) to Petruchio's powerfully gendered "Another way I have to man my haggard" (4.1.193), the play traditionally codes the literary feminine and the rational or philosophic masculine, but it also obsessively situates its own reception within the very disruption of sexual difference that it performs, as if the university were the bankside, brothel-bound theater *tamed*, disembodied (alma mater) or masculinized (ivory tower)—"To suck the sweets of sweet philosophy" (1.1.28). Whereas Kate's Bianca-like taming entails the wholesale *repression* of sexual difference, Bianca's Kate-like subversion of pedagogy coincides with its bawdy *return*:

> I am no breeching scholar in the schools,
> I'll not be tied to hours, and pointed times,
> But learn my lessons as I please myself.
> And to cut off all strife. . . .
>
> (3.1.18–21)[3]

So the difference between the theater and the university, from its earliest formulation in Plato to the present, is sexual difference. When falling under the power of music and meter, Socrates warns in *Ion*, poets are "like Bacchic maidens who draw milk and honey from the rivers when they are under the influence of Dionysus" (534b). Poems in the ideal Republic, in turn, must be strictly regulated, since "there is a danger that our guardians may be rendered too excitable and effeminate by them" (*Republic* 387b). Not surprisingly, then, Socrates' suggestion that "the doings of Kronos . . . had better be buried in silence" begins his epochal case for philosophy's difference from (and with) literature, leaving out what Hesiod's *Theogony* begins by leaving in—the difference, sexual difference, separating literature from philosophy.

Socrates thus *tames* literature into philosophy much as *The Taming of the Shrew* stages its own Neoplatonic untaming of the university (Petruchio) by the theater (Kate), beginning rather than ending with Lucentio's "Here let us breathe, and haply institute / A course of learning and ingenious studies" (1.1.8–9). So in Cervantes's equally representative *Don Quixote,* the illiterate Sancho Panza's allegiance to the over-read Quixote recapitulates, in reverse, Plato's faithful recording of the unwritten Socrates. On the one hand, Quixote's madness lives beyond the same veil of appearances as Socrates' transcendent vision, and somehow attains to a similar truth; on the other, the novel's Platonic inversion, like the play's, depends on the return or the untaming of a repressed sexual difference, as can be seen from the very first, and most famous, of Quixote's adventures, that of the windmills. Here the mock-epic backdrop explicitly recalls the Homeric literature ultimately condemned by Socrates, and the giant machines are likened to "Briareus." The magnification, too, is oedipal, the son's struggle with the father (the windmill) for possession of the peerless Dulcinea del Toboso, his lance broken by the intervening superego (the wind). For, if the difference between rational philosophy (Petruchio) and irrational rhapsody (Kate) is sexual difference (if literature, as Socrates asserts, effeminizes), then every adventure undergone by Quixote negotiates the same sexual impasse, since each entails the passage from one realm to the other. When Quixote and Sancho leave the windmills, for example, only the oedipal backdrop links this episode to the one just following, in which the knight confronts a group of travelers taking a Basque woman to her husband. Believing the woman a charmed and disguised Dulcinea, Quixote challenges the group. A Basque man appears, and he and Quixote fiercely join battle at full gallop as the first part of the first book of *Don Quixote* ends, colliding with a force that splits the narrative. When the dust settles, and the second part begins, Cervantes writes:

> In the first part of this history we left the valiant Basque and the famous Don Quixote with naked swords aloft [*con las espadas altas y desnudas*], on the point of dealing two such

furious downward strokes as, had they struck true, would have cleft both knights asunder from head to foot, and split them like pomegranates. At this critical point our delightful history stopped short and remained mutilated [*destroncada*], our author failing to inform us where to find the missing part.[4]

What Socrates represses in the name of an ideal Republic, Cervantes brings to the surface with all the force necessary to make a difference in, and for, the narrative, as well as the Republic; in "split them like pomegranates [*abrirían como una granada*]," a play on the last Arab stronghold at Granada further refigures one founding violence in the other. Like the absent frame in Shakespeare's play, the effeminizing difference suppressed by Socrates is, quite literally, "missing," even *miss*-ing, as in Donalbain's "What is amiss?" and, fresh from Duncan's "unsexing," Macbeth's "You are, and do not know it" (2.3.97). At the same time Cervantes directs his prologue to part 1 not just against "the swarm [*caterva*] of vain books of chivalry" (30) but, several pages earlier, against "Aristotle, Plato and the whole herd [*caterva*] of philosophers" (26)—one *caterva*, one *Cervantes*, reborn in the other. Ten years later, in the prologue to part 2, he answers the author of a slanderous preface to a pirated *Don Quixote* in similar terms, who had gone so far as to condemn Cervantes for the wound he received in the famous naval battle of Lepanto:

> What I cannot help resenting is that he upbraids me for being old and crippled, as if it were in my power to stop the passage of time, or as if the loss of my hand had taken place in some tavern, and not on the greatest occasion which any age, past, present, or future, ever saw or can ever hope to see. (467)

The mutilated text is now a maimed hand, a violent style; the hyperbole, "the greatest occasion which any age, past, present, or future, ever saw or can ever hope to see," is Quixote's.

Cervantes's novel thus subverts the language of philosophy with the language of literature through a return of this repressed sexual difference, just as, in *The Taming of the Shrew*, the language of the theater disrupts the language of the university. At either institutional extreme, traditional ascriptions of shrewishness to Socrates' wife, Xanthippe, correspond to equally speculative references to the shrewish behavior of Shakespeare's wife, Anne Hathaway.[5] So the closely related early comedy *Love's Labour's Lost* begins with the king of Navarre's "Our court shall be a little academe, / Still and contemplative in living art" (1.1.13–14), *emplotting* Plato's suppression of the effeminizing dangers of literature ("on pain of losing her tongue" [1.1.124]) and their return as theater, in this case as *Love's Labour's Lost*. From the play's hyper-alliterative title to Holofernes's "Of one sore I an hundred make by adding but one more L" (4.2.61), the more "more L," Herbert A. Ellis suggests, the more *moral*—"by adding but one *moral*" ("the king he is hunting the deer" [4.1.1]).⁶ For the more verbal pyrotechnics, the more *signifier-works,* the more the constative language of the Neoplatonic academy gives institutional rise to the radically performative discourse of the early modern theater, "in reason nothing," as Dumaine remarks of Berowne's non sequitur "The spring is near when green geese are a-breeding" (1.1.97–99), "something then in rhyme," as C. L. Barber draws the moral for *Love's Labour's Lost* and all of Shakespeare's green-world comedies: "The spring is near when green geese are a-breeding" (Navarre's "Vouchsafe to show the sunshine of your face, / That we (like savages) may worship it" [5.2.201–2]). So Armado's "l'envoy," "The fox, the ape, and the humble-bee / Were still at odds, being but three" (2.1.88–89), points the moral ("There's the moral" [86]) of the three sonneteers and Berowne's "Now step I *forth* to whip hypocrisy" (4.3.149)—Moth's "Until the goose came out of door, / Staying the odds by adding four" (90–91). For the more "more L," Armado's *l'envoy* affirms, the more *"elle"* (Costard's "I was taken with none, sir, I was taken with a damsel" [1.1.289–90]), and the more *elle,* finally, the more Elizabeth, from Boyet's "Queen Guinover of Britain" (4.1.123) and Nathaniel's "a title to Phoebe, to Luna, to the moon" (4.2.38) to Petruchio's hyperironic "Did ever Dian so become a grove / As Kate this chamber with her *princely* gait? / O be thou Dian and let her be Kate" (2.1.258–60).⁷ Hence the opening "Let fame, that all hunt after in their lives," which carries the obsessive alliteration of the title into the play, but hence, too, the closing songs of Winter and Spring ushered in by Don Armado's final "Holla! approach" (5.2.890), which points the play's moral by way of the same repeating *L*, and, following this medieval *conflictus* of the cuckoo and the owl, "the words of Mercury are harsh after the songs of Apollo."

In all four wanton instances—Holofernes's "sorel [sore *elle*]," Berowne's "geese" (prostitutes), Moth's "goose," and Armado's "owl" and "cuckoo" (cuckold)—patriarchy is confirmed but from Kate's antirational perspective, as if Berowne's "Light, seeking light, doth light of light beguile" (1.1.77) were the true moral, or "more *elle*" ("light in the light" [2.1.198]), of *Love's Labour's Lost*. For the more "more L," more *elle,* and more Elizabeth, the more *Will* ("a sharp wit matched with too blunt a will, / Whose edge hath power to cut, whose will still wills" [2.1.49–50])—the Shakespeare/Shrew alliteration, the "*Shre W.,*" whose elaborate signature-effect signs off, too, on the play's own "taming" by the state apparatus (the "academe") it ironically affirms. So Petruchio's "tailor," who is also Petruchio's "taler"— "Saving your tale, Petruchio . . . , Backare, you are marvelous forward" (2.1.71–73); "What, with my tongue in your tail?" (218); "Out of their saddles and into the dirt, and thereby hangs a tale" (3.2.57–58); "My widow says, thus she conceives her tale" (5.2.24)—discomfits both genders alike with the phallic cap ("Fie, fie, 'tis lewd and filthy. / Why, 'tis a cockle or a walnut-shell . . . / Away with it! come let me have a bigger" [4.3.66–68]) and bawdy gown ("Take up my mistress' gown to his master's use! / O fie, fie, fie!" [162–63]) that he has fashioned for Kate ("Error i' th' bill, sir, error i' th' bill!" [145]). In *Troilus and Cressida*, a play whose obvious affinities with *The Taming of the Shrew* go far beyond Petruchio's spaniel "Troilus" (4.1.150) or Lucentio's "*Hic ibat Simois; hic est Sigeia tellus*" (3.1.28), the autobiographical moral is only more explicit: the play is Cressida ("*This* is, and is not, Cressid!" [5.2.146]), the spectator Troilus, and the playwright Pandarus, who concludes the action by bringing just this self-authoring allegory to the surface: "Till then I'll sweat and seek about for eases, / And at that time bequeath you my diseases" (5.10.55–56).[8] In one of these later bequests, Imogen's midnight reading of "The Rape of Philomel" in *Cymbeline*—"I have read three hours then" (2.2.3)—similarly figures not just her plight but her play and its own three-hour "noting" by the Jachimo-like spectator: "One, two, three, time, time!" (51). For the play not only generates plot by untaming and taming female sexuality, as in *The Taming of the Shrew* and *Troilus and Cressida*, but duly records its own effeminized status as the Imogen-like object of the very patriarchal noting it celebrates. Across a corresponding sixteen year "gap" in time (Kronos), the bawdy ballads that the wandering rogue Autolycus sells his audience in the pastoral second half of *The Winter's Tale* ("Pins and poking-sticks of steel, / What maids lack from head to heel" [4.4.226–27]) Shakespeare sells his, miraculously transforming the Othello-like jealousy of Leontes and Mamillius for Hermione into the shared affection of Hermione and Perdita for Leontes ("Why, this is a passing merry one and goes to the tune of 'Two maids wooing a man'" [288–89]).

Sexual difference, in these ways, *centers* the plays—the difference, again, between Rome and Egypt, England and France, Montague and Capulet, Venice and Belmont, the court and the forest, the tragedies, finally, and the comedies—because it represents the difference, inside out, between the play and its audience, the stage and its reception. For it is across *this* difference, sexual difference, that the experience of attending the theater and returning home recapitulates the gendered movement from court to imaginary forest to court (and courtship) in comedies like *The Winter's Tale* ("Come on then, / And give't me in mine ear" [2.1.31–32]), *The Merchant of Venice* ("I am a tainted wether of the flock" [4.1.114]), and *A Midsummer Night's Dream* ("Marry, if he that writ it had played Pyramus, and hanged himself in Thisby's garter, it would have been a fine tragedy" [5.1.357–60]). In *The Taming of the Shrew* Shakespeare's revisionist-antirevisionist perspective, his perpetual upping of the "anti," closely resembles a pair of engravings reproduced in Barbara Freedman's book *Staging the Gaze: Postmodernism, Psychoanalysis, and Shakespearean Comedy:* Albrecht Dürer's woodcut from *Unterweisung der Messung* (1525) and M. C. Escher's *Print Gallery* (1956) (fig. 1). In Dürer's woodcut the taming of an effeminized nature by a patriarchal gaze corresponds to a literal, antirevisionist reading of Kate's conversion. From left to right the two hills in the window above the woman unironically yield to the potted plant in the window to the artist/spectator's right. In Escher's lithograph, by contrast, the lack of a closing frame on the right side of the canvas, like the lack of a closing frame for the Induction in the play, draws the viewer squarely into the picture, even as the onlooker's head literally rises into the frame. From this revisionist perspective the woman to the left of the engraver in Dürer's etching is now the diminutive woman in the window to the observer's right.

From (ideological) right to left it is therefore not surprising that postwar feminism should find in *The Taming of the Shrew*, which thematically recalls Dürer's engraving but structurally resembles Escher's *Print Gallery*, not just the patriarchal story to end all patriarchal stories but its most concentrated and overdetermined subversion—*The Shaming of the True.*[9] Though ironic readings of Kate's final speech reach back to comments by Constance O'Brien in 1886 and Margaret Webster in 1942, Nevill Coghill establishes the play's postwar revisionist tradition in 1950 by suggesting that the play's moral is "generously and charmingly asserted by Katerina at the end," adding: "it is a total misconception to suppose that she has been bludgeoned into it" (O'Brien's "it is all nonsense to talk as if this bit of merry comedy expresses Shakespeare's serious ideas of the proper relations between husband and wife").[10] A year after Coghill's remarks (and sixty-five years after O'Brien's) Harold Goddard argues still more forcefully that "*The Taming of the Shrew* . . . is possibly the most striking example among [Shakespeare's] early works of his love for so

Figure 1.
(above) Albrecht Dürer, woodcut from *Unterweisung der Messung* (1525).
From *The Complete Woodcuts of Albrecht Dürer*, ed. Willi Kurth (Mineola, N.Y.: Dover Publications, 1963).
(below) M. C. Escher, *The Print Gallery* (1956).

contriving a play that it should mean, to those who might choose to take it so, the precise opposite of what he knew it would mean to the multitude." According to Goddard, "why explain what is as clear, when you see it, as was Poe's Purloined Letter, which was skillfully concealed precisely because it was in such plain sight all the time" (68). Figuring the play's *too* obvious revisionism, "The Purloined Letter" here takes up the alliterating *L* of *Love's Labour's Lost* (the prefect's "it was all labor lost" [213]) while linking its own signifying desire to that of woman, even as Dupin's "the letter had been turned, as a glove, inside out" bawdily revisits Festes' "A sentence is but a chev'ril glove to a good wit. How quickly the wrong side may be turned outward!" (*Twelfth Night* [3.1.11–13]).[11]

Since Goddard's remarks, an increasingly vocal appeal to the play's apparent "irony" characterizes the series of so-called revisionist readings, from Richard Hosley's "Kate's speech . . . was probably, without denial of the basic validity of its doctrine, as susceptible to an ironic interpretation in Shakespeare's day as in our own" (1964) to Coppélia Kahn's "[the play's] greatest irony [is that it] . . . satisfies not woman herself in the person of the shrew, but male attitudes toward women" (1975) and Roger L. Cox's "to call Kate's final speech 'exaggerated and ironic' is . . . like calling Falstaff 'obese,' as if the casual observer might not have noticed that he tended to be rather plump" (1991).[12] For revisionist readers Kate's final speech simply humors Petruchio, but for antirevisionist readers, by sharp contrast, Kate's final speech simply "humors" Petruchio (i.e., amuses or pleases him), as Robert B. Heilman first counters in *"The Taming Untamed, or, The Return of the Shrew"* (1966): "we have domesticated a free-swinging farce and made it into a brittlely ironic closet drama, the voice of a woman's world in which apron strings, while proclaiming themselves the gentle badge of duty, snap like an overseer's lash."[13] Following Heilman's "untaming" of Kate's controversial "mating," antirevisionist appeals to the play's literalness (and criticism's performativity) include Richard Levin's "the many ironic readings of [*Henry V*] and *The Taming of the Shrew* and *The Merchant of Venice* can also be explained in this way. . . . To remain worthy of our worship, the idol's meaning must be changed, like that of our other sacred texts, to conform with current beliefs" (1979); Peter Saccio's "I cannot agree with the common modern view that seeks to revise the plain doctrine of Kate's last speech under the all-saving name of irony. . . . [Such readings] ignore the difference between local verbal ironies and the massive irony of intent extending through forty-four lines" (1984); and Camille Wells Slights's "Petruchio certainly demands that Kate submit to his will, but we know, as she does, that he won't step on her hand. Shakespeare, then, does not ironically subvert the patriarchal power structure portrayed in *The Taming of the Shrew*" (1993).[14] From one ironic extreme (Kate) to the other (Petruchio) *The Taming of the Shrew*, still more ironically, serves no longer as a pretext but a prototype for the critical debate it engenders, one that alternately tames and untames, from Petruchio to Kate, the play—hence the more recent "beyond-revisionist" readings for which even the play's irony, in the final analysis, proves ironic, as in Jonathan Hall's "when I refer to [Kate's] flight from determination through 'inward dialogism' as *ironic*, I certainly do not mean the kind of stabilized irony which supports a definitely satirical kind of feminist reading" (1995) or Natasha Korda's "I do not mean to suggest (following the play's so-called revisionist readers) that Kate's speech should be read ironically, as evidence of her deceit, any more than (with its anti-revisionist readers) as evidence of her 'true' submission" (1996).[15]

Thus it is also not surprising, in connection with the return of a parallel repressed in *The Taming of the Shrew*, that postwar critiques of the play should ultimately move beyond the binarisms of revisionist/antirevisionist to find in Kate's final moral not just the taming story to end all taming stories but, as Kahn is among the first to propose, a surprisingly sophisticated staging ground for feminism's own elaborate cross-dressings of literature, gender, and power, as in the following remarks by Karen Newman:

> The theatrically constructed frame in which Sly exercises patriarchal power and the dream in which Kate is tamed undermine the seemingly eternal nature of those structures by calling attention to the constructed character of the representation rather than veiling it through mimesis. The foregrounded female protagonist of the action and her powerful annexation of traditionally male discursive domains distances us from that system by exposing and displaying its contradictions.[16]

So in postwar feminism, Newman contends,

> we need a different kind of textual intercourse, a promiscuous conversation of many texts, early modern elite and non-elite, historical records and ideological discourses, contemporary theory and popular culture, that puts into play the "literary,"

the "historical," "gender," as relations and positions rather than static categories. . . . (146)

Shakespeare is immediately essential to this "textual intercourse" because, as Valerie Traub observes, "the homoeroticism of Shakespearean comedy transverses 'masculine' and 'feminine' sites, challenging the binary language of identity by which *we* normalize erotic desire."[17] Regarding the corresponding fate of postwar feminism in the literary academy, Freedman notes in *Staging the Gaze* how "psychoanalytic and deconstructive approaches that demonstrate that we cannot escape the text, the symbolic, or ideology remind us of the means by which Kate is encouraged to believe that she can never escape the theater of difference in which she exists"—Gremio's "My cake is dough" (5.1.140).[18] Outside the academy feminism occasions a resistance strikingly akin to the antitheatrical prejudice of the early 1580s and beyond, as Jean Howard remarks of representative tracts by Stephen Gosson (1579), Anthony Munday (1580), and Phillip Stubbes (1583): "the social change which the antitheatrical rhetoric was struggling to manage produced fear and anger and incomprehension in many quarters, not only among the powerful who felt they had something to lose if servants wore velvet or women asserted independence from masculine control of their dress and speech."[19] Within the university, as both Freedman and Newman affirm, Kate's subversion of gender initiates a "domestic and domesticating quarrel," as Fineman remarks in "The Turn of the Shrew," that literally refigures the university in the theater and the theater in the university (Heilman's "we have domesticated a free-swinging farce and made it into a brittlely ironic closet drama").[20] For if sexual difference is "a linchpin," as Foucault contends, "an especially dense transfer point for relations of power . . . endowed with the greatest instrumentality," feminism and theater in *The Taming of the Shrew* mark an equally dense "transfer point" whose corresponding eclipse of patriarchal *sun* by Elizabethan *moon* ("Now by my mother's son, and that's myself, / It shall be moon, or sun, or what I list" [4.6.6–7]) literally transforms the early modern university of Lucentio's opening speech into social and political theater.[21]

In her book *Feminism and Theater* Sue-Ellen Case proposes that the theater itself represents the taming site upon which Western culture is significantly founded, particularly in the *Oresteia*, which "Simone de Beauvoir and Kate Millet characterize . . . as the mythological rendering of a patriarchal takeover."[22] Overtaking patriarchy, Shakespeare and feminism register a similar return of this repressed, in the theater but also in the university, complicating while placating, like Cleopatra, the patriarchal desire delimited or defined by this struggle over sexual difference—the *am*, finally, in Petruchio's drive to "tame" ("For I am he am born to tame you, Kate" [2.1.276]). For from the theater to the university the ubiquitous comic play of feminized *O* and patriarchal *thing* in the truly self-canceling moral of *The Taming of the Shrew*, "O this learning, what a thing it is!" (1.2.159), makes the play itself the lesson, and the playwright the Petruchio, of Hortensio's (and the spectator's) "Then hast thou taught Hortensio to be unto-ward" (4.5.79)—Lucentio's "fair Padua, nursery of arts" (1.1.2). So *teaching*, the main part of feminist criticism of *The Taming of the Shrew* works to make Kate's final speech not more but less "domesti-cated." For the difference between doing and saying in the theater (dra-matic irony) is also the difference, sexual difference, between saying and doing in the university (Socratic irony). In Shakespeare's England the very exclusion of actresses, in sharp contrast to their presence on the Continental stage, partly reflects the powerful shaping influence of the all-male universities of Cambridge and Oxford on the emerging national theater, Petruchio "Kated." Shakespeare's strong female char-acters such as Kate thus strike strong blows against the *academy*, admitting or accepting such women even when, especially when, "tamed." From the frame to the play, in turn, the irony entails first an irony of form; in *The Merchant of Venice* the ironic (revisionist) read-ing of Shylock's trial scene nowhere more compellingly inheres than when, in a wholly other context and on the level of form, Bassanio rejects the gold casket because "In law, what plea so tainted and cor-rupt / But, being seasoned with a gracious voice, / Obscures the show of evil?" (3.2.75–77), adding: "Look on beauty, / And you shall see 'tis purchased by the weight" (88–89). In *The Taming of the Shrew* a still more elaborate formal irony extends the play's patriarchal moral to its own Petruchio-like reception in much the way that a certain com-mercial self-consciousness joins Shakespeare to Shylock in *The Mer-chant of Venice*, or Shakespeare to Pandarus in *Troilus and Cressida*. Hence the final spelling of *shrow* for *shrew* in the closing couplet of *The Taming of the Shrew*, not for the rhyme but for the signature pun on *show*—as a parting remark, like Puck's "Give me your hands" or Pandarus's "And at that time bequeath you my diseases," to an audi-ence reaching beyond the *thou*, Petruchio, who has already grandly exited on "God give you good night!":

Hortensio: Now go thy ways, thou hast tamed a curst shrow.
Lucentio: 'Tis a wonder, by your leave, she will be tamed so.

The Pragmatist Dilemma: *Henry V*

Now and at moments of extreme intellectual turmoil such as fifth-century Athens or eighteenth-century Europe, the history of philosophy has taken special interest in the theatrical nature of all philosophical systems, of which pragmatism is the quintessential expression. For the core principle of pragmatism, like the core principle of theater, is that there are no core principles, only interventions. All truths are local and contingent, even—especially—this one. All descriptions, in turn, even scientific descriptions, possess a merely normative value, as Richard Rorty contends in a recent body of work that itself pragmatically mingles a certain Americanized Jamesianism with Saussurean semiotics, Husserlian intentionality, Foucauldian archaeology, Derridean deconstruction, Davidsonian positivism, Darwinian naturalism, Freudian determinism, and Nietzschean subjectivism: "[It] has been central to what I have been saying . . . that the world does not provide us with any criterion of choice between alternative metaphors, that we can only compare languages or metaphors with one another, not with something beyond language called 'fact.'"[1] According to Rorty, "about two hundred years ago, the idea that truth was made rather than found began to take hold of the imagination of Europe" (3), an idea that replaced "intrinsic nature" (4), "the 'intrinsic nature of reality'" (8), and even "the intrinsic nature of nature" (16) with a vision of "new forms of life constantly killing off old forms—not to accomplish a higher purpose, but blindly" (19). In this dogma-eat-dogma world the bottom or battle line is language, and language makes Rorty's version of pragmatism especially "postmodern": "what Hegel describes as a process of spirit gradually becoming self-conscious of its intrinsic nature is better described as the process of European linguistic practices changing at a faster and faster rate" (7).

In two books on Shakespeare and pragmatism published in 1992–93, Terence Hawkes's *Meaning by Shakespeare* and Lars Engle's *Shakespearean Pragmatism*, Shakespeare's poetry and plays obviously fall outside the two hundred–year history of pragmatism proposed by Rorty, but Hamlet's "there is nothing either good or bad, but thinking makes it so" (2.2.249–50) already underlies Rorty's "what was glimpsed at the end of the eighteenth century was that anything could be made to look good or bad, important or unimportant, useful or useless, by being redescribed" (7). "The conversation," Hawkes pragmatically affirms, "albeit of a harsher, more overtly political nature than Rorty allows, continues."[2] For Hawkes *The Mousetrap* in *Hamlet* "could hardly be bettered as an instance of that process and a measure of its potential impact. There are no essential, transcendental meanings here. An intention to 'mean mischief' is precisely the earnest of a commitment to material political intervention. . . . On this basis, *miching malicho* means 'taking part'" (6). In *Shakespearean Pragmatism* Engle similarly argues that Shakespeare remains "anti-transcendental; he locates the power to confer value and accept truth in social economies; and he is interested in social experimentation. His plays dramatize the uncertainties in experience which the new science and philosophy of the later seventeenth century sought to contain, and which twentieth-century pragmatists acknowledge" (227–28).

Pragmatism thus possesses a decidedly Shakespearean character, but so, Hawkes suggests in a final chapter on "Bardbiz," does the culture, both in the United Kingdom, with special reference to Hugh H. Grady's book *The Modernist Shakespeare: Critical Texts in a Material World*, and in the United States, with similar reference to Michael Bristol's *Shakespeare's America, America's Shakespeare*. On either shore "a chilling thesis emerges: the interpretation of Shakespeare and the interpretation of [Anglo-]American political culture are mutually determining practices" (152), as the twin examples of Lincoln's assassination and Melville's *Moby-Dick* suffice to illustrate. For here, across a fifteen year gap of time from 1850 to 1865, important Shakespearean transformations of history into literature (Melville) and literature into history (Lincoln) mark themselves the properly literary-historical extremes of the Civil War that divides them, from John Wilkes Booth's Caesarean "Sic semper tyrannis" to Ahab's final "thou damned whale! *Thus*, I give up the spear!"—Othello's "I took by the throat the circumcised dog / And smote him—thus" (5.2.355–56).[3] The sighting, Ahab's of the whale and Booth's along the gun barrel, is a citing—"thou damned *Will!*" again, "*Thus*, I give up the *Shakespeare.*" So Borges names his collection of short stories *Labyrinths* precisely when recasting Booth's dramatic leap from history to the stage, as if this particular passage opened onto something like the narrative's own literary-historical *minotaur:*

He thinks that, before having been Fergus Kilpatrick, Fergus Kilpatrick was Julius Caesar. He is rescued from these circular labyrinths by a curious finding, a finding which then sinks him into other, more inextricable and heterogeneous labyrinths: certain words uttered by a beggar who spoke with Fergus Kilpatrick the day of his death were prefigured by Shakespeare in the tragedy *Macbeth*. That history should have copied history was already sufficiently astonishing; that history should copy literature was inconceivable.[4]

In Lincoln's assassination history similarly "copies" literature, which in turn copies history in Lincoln's own "performance" of *Macbeth* five days before his assassination on a return trip aboard the *River Queen* from the captured Confederate capital of Richmond:

> On Sunday, April 9th, we were streaming up the Potomac. That whole day the conversation dwelt upon literary subjects. Mr. Lincoln read to us for several hours passages taken from Shakespeare. Most of these were from "Macbeth," and, in particular, the verses which follow *Duncan's* assassination. I cannot recall this reading without being awed in the remembrance, when *Macbeth* becomes king after the murder of *Duncan*, he falls a prey to the most horrible torments of mind.[5]

In "Duncan's assassination" and Macbeth's "torments of mind," Booth's "Sic semper tyrannis" already replays Lincoln's own "Here may you see the tyrant" (5.8.27) within the very institutional refashioning of Anglo-American culture by meta-Shakespearean drama at the heart of Hawkes's "Bardbiz." For if Shakespearean drama, as René Girard presents it, variously situates the Roman and English civil wars within a culture-wide "crisis of no difference" that only the hero's sacrifice, as such, can resolve, the American Civil War resolves its nation-forging crisis of no difference by turning into Shakespearean drama.[6]

Which brings us to the pragmatist dilemma, and to *Henry V*. For if the play, as Engle contends, "presents royal legitimacy in pragmatic terms" (108), it also projects deep-seated cultural anxieties and contradictions onto its perspective-like hero. As early as 1919, in the wake of World War I, Gerald Gould argues in "A New Reading of *Henry V*" that "the play is ironic," but it was not until post-Vietnam America that Norman Rabkin's "Either/Or: Responding to *Henry V*" (1981) offered a sustained account of the play's double king.[7] "In

Henry V," Rabkin argues, "Shakespeare created a work whose ultimate power is precisely the fact that it points in two opposite directions, virtually daring us to choose one of the two opposed interpretations it requires of us" (34). Henry's valiant discovery of the traitors
Scroop, Grey, and Cambridge thus sandwiches between the death of
his own bosom consort, Falstaff, whom Henry has similarly betrayed;
the pardon that Henry extends earlier in the scene to a nameless man
"who railed against our person" guiltily glosses over the very pardon
denied Falstaff: "We consider / It was excess of wine that set him on, /
And on his more advice we pardon him" (2.2.41–43). Deepening the
perspective, Henry's most reverent moment of prayer during his
appeal for victory on the eve of Agincourt thinly veils over his most
demonic or delusional desire:

> O God of battles, steel my soldiers hearts,
> Possess them not with fear! Take from them now
> The sense of reck'ning, if th' opposèd numbers
> Pluck their hearts from them.
>
> (4.1.289–92)

Here "steel my soldiers' hearts" barely represses a deeper, far more
duplicitous design—namely, "*steal* my soldiers' hearts." All the verbs
that follow *steel—Possess, Take, Pluck their hearts*—repeat while
repressing this contrary reading, only to have it surface one last time
at Pistol's parting "To England will I steal, and there I'll steal" (5.1.87).
Even Henry's "O God of battles," revisiting the Chorus's opening "O
for a muse of fire," both echoes and undercuts the French Constable's
earlier "Dieu de batailles!" (3.5.15). For if Rabkin's almost Kierkegaardian "Either/Or" does not include the silent *e* for *a* of "steel my
soldiers' hearts," or even the more properly audible *p* for *b* of
Fluellen's Welshing comparison of his kinsman to "Alexander the
Pig" (4.7.13), as David Quint elaborates it, the essay nevertheless ends:
"For a unique moment in Shakespeare's work ambiguity is the *heart*
of the matter, the single most important fact we must confront in
plucking out the mystery of the world we live in" (62; italics added).[8]

    The play and its pragmatist revision thus complicate the fable-of-
the-bees jingoism of Rabkin's "duck-rabbit" hero (34)—now Machi-
avellian self-scheming prince, now "this star of England" (epi.6), "the
mirror of all Christian kings" (2.cho.6). For in this case the shaping
influence of contemporary history extends all the way to Henry's
identification with the ongoing campaign of Essex in Ireland:

The Mayor and all his brethren in best sort . . .
Go forth and fetch their conquering Caesar in,
As by a lower but by loving likelihood,
Were now the general of our gracious Empress,
As in good time he may, from Ireland coming,
Bringing rebellion broached on his sword,
How many would the peaceful city quit
To welcome him!

(5.cho.25–34)

Syntactically (and even tactically), "Go forth and fetch their conquering Caesar in" potentially includes "The mayor and all his brethren"
among the conquered, even as Essex momentarily returns "Bringing
rebellion," a perspectival transformation of ongoing historical violence that probably culminates in Troilus's ringing

do not give advantage
To stubborn critics, apt without a theme
For depravation, to square the general sex
By Cressid's rule

(*Troilus and Cressida*, 5.2.130–33)

—to square the general *Essex*, again, by Elizabeth's rule.[9] So Troilus's
equally ringing "What's aught but as 'tis valued?" (2.2.52) pragmatically affirms the same radical relativism as Hamlet's own wartime
determination, Hawkes himself might allow, to "know a hawk from a
hand-saw" (2.2.379).

Beginning, then, with the Irish backdrop for the action in *Henry V*,
in both Hawkes's and Engle's Shakespearean pragmatisms of 1992–93
a corresponding historical contradiction characterizes the recently
concluded Gulf War in Iraq. In the play Henry's various antagonists
and alter egos are all reimagined versions of himself, the former Harry,
by the smallest measure of a letter—*Har*fleur, the French *Her*ald,
"*Her*od's bloody-hunting slaughter-men" (3.3.41), the now *meta*mani-
acal "*stea*l my soldiers' *hear*ts," and, finally, "Rex Angliae et *Hae*res
Franciae" (5.2.341–42); in the war, which brought the coinage *friendly
fire* into common usage, George Bush similarly urged Iraqis to rise up
against the dictator "and join the family of peace-loving nations,"
nations then embarked, in equally self-reflexive fashion, on the
fiercest saturation bombing of a largely defenseless army in military
history. When, following the tragic bunker bombing in Baghdad,

White House spokesperson Marlin Fitzwater lamented that "Saddam Hussein is not above sacrificing civilians to further his war aims," that is exactly what the allied forces had just done—sacrificed civilians to further their war aims. When, on the other hand, groups of Iraqi soldiers were captured, or even rescued, by allied troops, many chanted, "George Bush! George Bush!" In the play, too, colonial violence engenders a properly oedipal anxiety ("Once more unto the breach, dear friends, once more" [3.1.1]) that underwrites Katherine's emblematic English anatomy lesson—"d'hand, de fingre, de mailès [de *males*]"—"De nailès [de*nials*], madame"—by drawing the line on translation at *"le count"* (3.4.52). Here the missing letter, the "wooden O" or "cockpit" within which all of the action unfolds, calls forth the play's own signifying desire, a Henryesque desire *to* signify (the V in *Henry V*, the O in "O for a Muse of fire," *breached* [1.cho.1–13]). In the war Bush's unique pronunciation of Saddam Hussein's first name to rhyme with *madame, Sad-dam*, similarly leaves out of the signifying loop the one signifier whose repression constitutes that movement—*Sodom, sodomy, Saddam Hussein*, but also *Sodom and Gomorrah*, Middle Eastern cities destroyed from the sky for just that transgression. As Jonathan Goldberg remarks of widespread wartime associations of *Saddam* and *sodomy:*

> even as "America" is invited to perform an act—Saddam's act—that act must be read and done otherwise. . . . If Saddam is blasted away, if the homosexual is destroyed, it would be impossible ever to suppose that proper male aggression could be misrecognized as sodomy. First, these images misrecognize Saddam's aggression as sodomy, then they claim the rights of aggression.[10]

Bush, slang for the same effeminizing lack, further situates in the proper name an emulous rivalry of biblical coevals—Saddam-Bush—as a struggle born of, and structured around, this same maternal loss (the "Gulf," again, underlying "the mother of all battles" but also the bizarre "baby milk factory," complete with signs in English, that allied planes allegedly destroyed as a chemical weapons plant). From the play to the war, then, the absurd casualty estimates at Agincourt—twenty-nine on the English side, "ten thousand" on the French (4.8.80–106)—underscore the routine rewriting of history by myth-minded chroniclers, but official casualty estimates in the Gulf War—one hundred and forty-seven on the allied side, two hundred and fifty thousand on the Iraqi side—are actually more absurd, as if the war were the play, the way the play was the war, literalized.

From Ireland to Iraq, the theater dramatizes the same heightened relativism, skepticism, and militarism as the criticism, adding somewhat ironic support to Engle's contention that "late sixteenth-century England and late twentieth-century America *may be* akin in that both cultures were hospitable to skepticism about the truths provided by certainty-producing institutions" (49; italics added). For, taken pragmatically, Shakespearean drama enacts an ongoing historical violence that returns to the criticism ("Cry, 'God for Harry, England, and Saint George!'" [3.1.34]), a displacement that receives further personal point in the gloss Hawkes gives to the following lines from *Coriolanus:*

> like an eagle in a dovecote, I
> Fluttered your Volscians in Corioles.
> Alone I did it.
>
> (5.6.114–16)

Fluttered is a third folio emendation of the first folio's *flattered*, a revision Hawkes would reject as "to some degree the semantic fulcrum" of a long-standing but misdirected reading of Caius Martius as "the heroic embattled individualist." In Hawkes's view, "'flattered' . . . suggests a much more complex interactive engagement with the Volscians than the imperiously dismissive 'fluttered'" (55), but even here a somewhat more fanciful substitution of *Hawkes* for *eagle* already works to heighten, or simply "flatter," the more immediate individuality of the criticism, a substitution perhaps less alarming in a book with the temerity to call Harley Granville-Barker's seemingly quietistic wartime *King Lear* "a dog that didn't bark" (133), and from the author (Hawkes) of *Shakespeare's Talking Animals*. Recalling the *e* and *a* in *steel my soldiers' hearts*, the *u* and *a* in *fluttered/flattered* literalize the difference not just between two opposing readings of the action and its overdetermined hero but between the play and its ongoing reception: "Coriolanus the individualist, the single subject, *the author of himself,* would certainly 'flutter' the Volscians. But to 'flatter' them subtly undercuts and questions that role. In a play in which that kind of 'flattering' relationship is made an issue throughout, there is a sense in which *the heart of the text* lies here" (56; italics added). Hence the swan-song metamorphosis of Hawkes's central chapter, "Take Me to Your Leda," and its closing ornithological, Anglo-Gallic dogfight *over* (above and about) the swan-of-Avon/upstart-Crow Bard, if still under the aegis of the 1596 spear-shaking, pen-flying falcon on his father's coat of arms and its almost Spenserian *non sanz droict:* "if we wish Leda to become our leader we can hardly also hope to remain, as the French might say, *du côté de chez Swan*" (78).

Hawkes's *Meaning by Shakespeare* thus defers as well to an ultimate meaning by history, like the one underwriting the 1942 skirmish between L. C. Knights and F. R. Leavis over *Measure for Measure:* "Leavis's self-appointed role in *Scrutiny* as Shakespeare's lieutenant, charged with the strict enforcement of the Bard's meaning" (67). A quarter century before, during the formation of modern English studies at Cambridge in 1917, Hawkes posits a still more direct causal relation between criticism and its historical moment:

> The study of "creative," "poetic" writing—literature—institutionalized in the new academic subject called English, was also the product of a conflict, but a much bloodier one. In the words of F. I. Lucas,
>
>> It was . . . in March 1917 while the German armies were falling back to the Hindenberg Line, while Russia was tottering into Revolution and America preparing for war, that at Cambridge members of the Senate met to debate the formation of an English Tripos. (68)

Hawkes further notes of Granville-Barker's World War II *King Lear* that Parliament's culminating Emergency Powers Bill of 22 May 1940 came "right in the middle of the run of the play" (133), even if a chronology earlier in the chapter makes clear that the bill was passed two days before the close of the play's forty-day engagement. The reading is therefore relevant—the primal scene as it were of English academic studies and modern Shakespearean criticism turned wartime recasting of the tremendous historical energies contained and released by Shakespearean drama—but its *post hoc ergo propter hoc* literary history is also literally *forced*, like Knights's account of *Measure for Measure*, of which Hawkes writes: "I shrink from the bald proposal that he saw himself as a compromised Claudio anxious, despite the evidence, to justify his crime" (67). Hence what might be called "the pragmatist dilemma," for the core principle of pragmatism, that all philosophical systems and individual assertions are historically determined effects of a larger cultural and institutional dialogue, necessarily takes in the principle, itself one more Shakespearean trope in a Nietzschean "army of metaphors": "the philosopher's [Wittgenstein's] initial reconnaissance . . . draws withering tracer fire" (69). When Hawkes remarks of the much-contrasted cinematic versions of *Henry V* that "Olivier's film addresses the Allied invasion of Normandy in 1944 and—perhaps more obliquely—Kenneth Branagh's film engages with the current carnage of Belfast" (147), the same goes for his own moving perspective on the plays and the two World Wars, Vietnam, the Falklands, Ireland, Iraq, and the all-embracing relativistic, even Heisenbergian, Cold War.

So *propped*, the great truth of pragmatism—that all ideational assertions are culturally relative, including this one—is therefore false, and therefore true, and therefore false, since the foundation on which it rests is performative rather than semantic. In the process its unique take on the famous liar's paradox, "All pragmatists are relativists, said the pragmatist," further complicates pragmatism because the democracy of pluralistic perspectives it celebrates also represents the most autocratic and, from ancient Greece to postmodern America, the most imperialistic of all political attitudes. Hence, democracy can be resisted, but such resistance, of course, is its supreme expression, self-determination itself, even as the democratic power structure strikingly recalls the royalist dynamic in Hawkes's suggestion that "the King, the virtual fount of social, political and spiritual unity here [*sic*] reveals himself to be the actual cause of cataclysmic, boundary-drawing division" (123–24).[11] As Rooney proposes in *Seductive Reasoning*, postmodern academic pluralism similarly replicates postwar American populism, which replicates postwar American imperialism:

> The very notion of pluralistic society is often identified with the United States as such, and, simultaneously, it is consistently associated with U.S. foreign policy. One can gloss this colloquial usage in a personal inflection as: "This is a free country. I can do (or say or believe) whatever I please." But the idiom also appears in presidential speeches on the need for "political pluralism" in Central America and in *New York Times* articles describing the National Endowment for Democracy with headlines that announce: "Missionaries for Democracy: U.S. Aid for Global Pluralism," and "U.S. Pays for Pluralism." (18–19)

Like the pluralism it underwrites, pragmatism therefore returns to the "theatrical situation" in *Henry V*, even as Cornel West's depiction of the pragmatist in *The American Evasion of Philosophy: A Genealogy of Pragmatism* could be Shakespeare's: "The pragmatists' preoccupation with power, provocation, and personality—in contrast, say, to grounding knowledge, regulating instruction, and promoting tradition—signifies an intellectual calling to administer to a confused populace caught in the whirlwinds of societal crisis."[12] So from the opening signature scene of *1 Henry IV*, which begins "So shaken as we are" and ends "I will, my liege" (1.1.108), through the close of the second scene on Hal's "Redeeming time when men think least I will" (1.2.217) and his virtual moment of epiphany ("I do, I will" [2.4.457]) to the final exchange of gloves between Henry and Williams (William S., William Shakespeare) in *Henry V* and the epilogue's "This star of England" (6), whose only real antecedent is "Our bending author" (2), Shakespeare also administers "to a confused populace caught in the whirlwinds of societal crisis" ("To England *will I* steal, and there I'll [*isle*] steal").[13] West's pragmatist intervention in "the Western philosophical conversation initiated by Plato" (5) is thus theatrical (and, in "Western," autobiographical), in much the way that his "attempt to explain America to itself at a particular historical moment" (5) already recasts Hamlet's "to hold as 'twere the mirror up to nature: to show . . . the very age and body of the time his form and pressure" (3.2.22–24).

Like Hal's "Redeeming time," Hamlet's "very age and body of the time" thus speaks as well to an important temporality joining pragmatism (whose utterances are acts) and theater (whose acts are utterances) to history (whose utterances are once again acts). In the case of Shakespeare's most notorious pragmatist, Richard III, "the time is out of joint" (*Hamlet*, 1.5.188) precisely because the violence at the center of the play distorts but also disrupts, even destroys, time—Hamlet's "By heaven, I'll make a ghost of him that lets me" (1.5.85) turned Richard's "by St. Paul, / I'll make a corse of him that disobeys" (1.2.36–37):

> *Richard:* Tell the clock there. Give me a calendar.
>   Who saw the sun today?
> *Ratcliffe:*   Not I, my lord.
> *Richard:* Then he disdains to shine; for by the book
>   He should have braved the East an hour ago.
>   (5.3.276–80)

So Macbeth's "By th' clock 'tis day, / And yet dark night strangles the travelling lamp" (2.4.6–7) recasts the founding violence of Kronos at the beginning of Hesiod's *Theogony*, extending from "by the book" to "By th' clock" the temporal distortion at issue in both passages to the thirteen years that divide them. In Richard's famous opening lines,

Now is the winter of our discontent
Made glorious summer by this son of York,

Now tells an audience what it wants to know ("What time is it?") but then almost immediately changes from "winter" to "glorious summer," again superimposing the temporal displacement described in the lines over their real-time reception. So in the echoing first lines of sonnet 33,

Full many a glorious morning have I seen
Flatter the mountain tops with sovereign eye,

a momentary temporal marker ("Full many a glorious morning") becomes, instead, the direct object of "I have seen full many a glorious morning flatter the mountain tops with sovereign eye" (Booth 186).[14] Richard's next two lines,

And all the clouds that low'r'd upon our house
In the deep bosom of the ocean buried,

continue the opening *Now* to the moment of his fall, as if precisely no time had elapsed:

The sun will not be seen to-day.
The sky doth frown and low'r upon our army.

(5.3.184–85)

Closing the circle, the final couplet begins:

Now civil wounds are stopped, peace lives again:
That she may long live here, God say amen!

"Born," he tells us in his opening speech, "before my time," Richard embodies pragmatism as Rorty represents it, which in turn embraces Richard *because* the violence he performs is always "now," and to the now. Short-circuiting the time separating Richmond's "the bloody dog is dead" (5.5.2) and Macduff's "the time is free" (5.9.21), Shakespearean drama delimits pragmatism by creating a subject composed not merely of but *by* history—the history play, finally, as pragmatism in its purest form.

All of which means, in connection with post-1968, post-Vietnam criticism and Shakespeare's *Henry V*, that the radical skepticism characterizing the theater still more radically animates the academy, from "Now is the winter of our discontent" to "Now is the time for all good men to come to the aid of their country." Traditionally, the university works to suppress the violent antifoundationalism or nonessentialism of the theater, but the unprecedented postwar value of pragmatism itself signals an institutional leveling of playhouse and schoolhouse, performance and paraphrase. In an influential essay on so-called new pragmatism in his book *Is There a Text in This Class?* Stanley Fish similarly notes of *Coriolanus,* the man and the play, that each projects onto history the activist force inherent in pragmatist discourse, since *Coriolanus* "is about what the theory is about, language and its power: the power to make the world rather than mirror it, to bring about states of affairs rather than report them, to constitute institutions rather than (or as well as) serve them."[15] Echoing Terry Eagleton on the ideological blindspots of neopragmatism, Gary Wihl notes of Fish's essay how the hero's notorious "I banish you" becomes the pragmatist's equally defiant "I banish 'theory,'" and even, according to Wihl, "I banish you, me, and everybody."[16] For, like the animalistic world of pragmatism invoked by Hawkes, Engle, Hegel, Eagleton, Rabkin, Granville-Barker, Rorty, Gould, Fish, Wihl, and Shakespeare, "theater," to quote Engle, "does not simply show audiences themselves, it explains them to themselves by allowing them to witness and partake in an experiment in the active evaluation of ideas, habits, and institutions" (55). So "barks," in any case, the pragmatist dogma: "Now, now!"—but only because so "roars," within the same perspectival *Mousetrap,* the pragmatist *line:* "Now!" For the moment that anchors meaning in pragmatist philosophy necessarily anchors the philosophy, which in turn refashions the theater, from "Follow, follow!" seventeen lines into the Chorus's speech before Harfleur (3.cho.17) to Henry's "On, on" seventeen lines into his (3.1.17), as Michael Goldman observes.[17] From Ireland to Iraq, the "naked aggression" (Bush) of Henry's (and Bush's) "cockpit" (the Dolphin's "my horse is my mistress" [3.3.44]) returns to the criticism's own Anglo-American posturing—"the eagle," as Bishop Ely points Hawkes's anagrammatical moral, "England" (1.2.169). Engle's *Shakespearean Pragmatism* thus ends, as perhaps it must, with not just its most but its least self-referential moment, an acknowledgment that "this book, of course, is only another manifestation of that ongoing process" (228)—the "continuous process of meaning-making," as Hawkes presents it in *Meaning by Shakespeare,* "to which all texts, as aspects of human culture, are always subject, and beyond which they may be conceivable but will remain ungraspable" (7).

"By heaven, thou echoest me": Lentricchia, *Othello*, de Man

In the current climate of literary studies one approaches *Othello* like a car with all the extras—mimetic desire, total specularity, the thematization of illusion, figural fratricide, actual suicide, complicated discourses on the nature of signs, of perception, of sexuality, all this against a background of Mediterranean intrigue and elaborate political power plays. It's all there, one is tempted to say. The Othello, and we buy. Temptation of this sort before a powerful and convincing fiction is perhaps not unusual in the case of *Othello,* since that is its theme.

In one sense the play arises out of a mistrust of the very theory it would seem so readily to invite. As the action begins, Iago is concerned that he has not been appointed Othello's lieutenant but also that Othello has selected, in his place, as *his* lieutenant or place-holder, "a great arithmetician, / One Michael Cassio, . . . / That never set a squadron in the field" (1.1.19–22). Accompanying Othello to Cyprus to defend it from a Turkish invasion, Iago carries out a revenge that is real enough—the false suggestion of Desdemona's adultery with Cassio, leading Othello to murder her and, discovering Iago's deception rather than Desdemona's, himself. But it is also the case that Iago's revenge, like Cassio's reputation, is entirely a function of figure, even of theory, dependent as it is upon a madly jealous Othello's systematic misreading of the events and characters that surround him. But Iago, too, is confined by this "arithmetic" not just in his failed promotion but in his wildest successes, and it is this question, the question of the limits of theory, within the play and with respect to it, that I want to take up in the following pages.

At the end of *Venus and Adonis,* the goddess, grieved at her lover's death, prophesies ill for love, which "shall be waited on with jealousy, / Find sweet beginning, but unsavory end" (1137–38). She then flies off to Cyprus in a chariot pulled by silver doves,

Holding their course to Paphos, where their queen
Means to immure herself and not be seen.

(1193–94)

This willed deception, which is also Iago's way, awaits Othello when
he, too, returns to Cyprus. In the opening scene Iago tells how Othello
has selected the untried Cassio for his lieutenant rather than himself,
"of whom his eyes had seen the proof / At Rhodes, at Cyprus"
(1.1.28–29). Here, a kind of circle leads from Othello's obliviousness
before Iago's "proof" back to Cyprus, and to Othello, enraged even to
madness and threatening Iago's life against the production of "ocular
proof." The whole thing is a B-grade Hollywood movie, or the extravagant travelogues parodied in Othello's "life-story," where, struggling
through a tremendous storm, the characters arrive at an island—and
there's a monster there. "The Fiction That Ate Cyprus," starring
Othello as Iago. This circle, from not seeing what is there to seeing
what isn't, brings one back but this time up to the eyes in fiction, and
in this sense it is a circle of reading, a map of textual identification.
The effects of this return on Othello, however, are far more extensive,
effects that must be read, first, against the circularity of Shakespeare's
so-called zero-person plays, of Iago's "I am not what I am" (1.1.63) or
Desdemona's "my lord is not my lord" (3.4.124), against the haywire
sexuality of Ophelia's "nothing" and Shakespeare's bawdy plays upon
O's, zeros, rings, and ciphers, even against the closure of representation into which so many characters playing characters, or plays characterizing plays, disappear, "raze" their likeness, in Edgar's typically
Hegelian pun, only to emerge once more as theater on Shakespeare's
"wooden O," or Cleopatra's "little O, the earth." Half-Iago, half-
Othello, Malvolio in *Twelfth Night* may be taken here as a typically
Shakespearean reader, in light of Stephen Booth's essay "The Audience as Malvolio," where "Malvolio [is] the preeminent example of a
character who mistakes evidence" in a play that perpetually means
more than it says, but also because, as comic scapegoat, Malvolio
brings the circle of comic marriage very close to, say, the revenge
cycles of tragedy.[1] Sir Toby Belch, Maria, and Fabian are in the bushes,
for, as Fabian points out, "Now is the woodcock near the gin" (*Twelfth
Night*, 2.5.83):

"I may command where I adore." Why, she may command
me: I serve her; she is my lady. . . . And the end—what should
that alphabetical position portend? If I could make that resemble something in me! Softly! M.O.A.I. (2.5.115–20)

"A fustian riddle," Fabian asides from the hedge, for the moment of Malvolio's duping, more overtly than Othello's, involves a breakdown of reading, an inability rather than a failure to read. The difference is no doubt slight, even unreadable; Othello, too, at the most crucial moment of his "conversion," experiences a similar inability to read, even to feel, when his breakdown takes the form of a seizure. In this sense Malvolio's transformation ("this wins him, liver and all") is somewhat less explicit, and perhaps more fortunate, than Othello's, falsely thinking he has won love rather than lost it, though one admits that at this point in Shakespeare's career it can be little fun to discover that reading is a process of resemblance and be stuck in a comedy, one that foregrounds, even more relentlessly than *Othello*, interpretation. Do what the play itself does so often, reverse the alphabetical position, and *M.O.A.I.* soon resembles very closely "something in" Malvolio: "I a 'O' am," the comic version, or inversion, as the case may be, of the tragic: "Now thou art an O without a figure. I am better than thou art now. I am a Fool, thou art nothing" (*King Lear*, 1.4.192–94).

When I say that jealousy offers a paradigm of critical responses to literary works I do not mean that what motivates it is envy. Of course, it may be that a certain Bloomian anxiety informs the reading of any work or author, who, usually deceased so many years as a condition of his or her canonization, leaves no outlet for the feeling except to dissipate it horizontally, where it emerges, often months or years later, as the proverbial rancor commonly associated with academic departments generally and certain philosophical schools, across interpretations now rather than across texts. But by jealousy-as-critical-paradigm I only mean the way jealousy involves constructing hugely imaginative scenarios that Othello reads, or reads awry, as involving him in ways they obviously do not, or should not. Othello's downfall proves the critic's livelihood: he must take seriously another individual's fiction, must believe it contains a truth about his life, his being. "Trifles light as air / Are to the jealous confirmations strong / As proofs of holy writ," Iago says (3.3.322–24). One of the amazing things about the notorious homosexual rendering of Iago's "the lusty Moor / Hath leaped into my seat" (2.1.295–96) is that the reading is as crazed and extravagant as Iago's suspicions of his wife, or just as justified. The image is especially arresting, of course, because the metaphor "leaped into my seat" is *theatrical*, inspired by Hamlet's more overtly self-reflexive "whiles memory holds a seat / In this distracted globe" (1.5.96–97). In responding to Othello, do we read into his life truths about our own because his life-story expresses them or because his life, as it is given to us and as readers or spectators of the play, is a story, one about the breakdown of defense after defense in the final submission to a fiction that, as Othello implies, swallows up all?

Iago says something quite extraordinary about the relation between representation and belief, which on second thought seems rather commonplace, when he says "Trifles light as air / Are to the jealous confirmations strong / As proofs of Holy Writ." The equation of jealousy and devotion reminds us that both involve submissions of faith to a particular narrative of events that remain, themselves, unseen. Associations of theater and religious ritual are familiar enough, particularly Shakespeare's theater, which begins, two centuries before, in the Mass. But Othello greatly limits the propriety of invoking the associations of a character's fate and Christ's, which occur in many of Shakespeare's tragedies but reach their peak just after *Othello*, in Coriolanus and Antony. It may be that Othello acts out a symbolic sacrifice in which the audience partakes, as Stanley Cavell suggests in a reading of *Coriolanus*, through a dense, biblical clustering of words–as–food imagery—the famous "Fable of the Belly," which satisfies a starving mob bent on overthrowing the Senate.[2] So Othello tells Brabantio of his travels, "of the Cannibals that each other eat," and how Desdemona would leave "the house affairs," as the citizens leave off rioting, and, "with a greedy ear / Devour up my discourse" (1.3.143–50). The "cannibalization" of Othello may represent a ritual of faith, as similar imagery does in plays like *Julius Caesar* and *King Lear*, but this displaced communion is not the only gloss given by Shakespeare to such imagery in *Othello*. The very darkness of the play would seem to insist upon an alternative model for the hero's undoing, if we are to take seriously the inevitable comparison of Shakespearean hero and bear—Othello's "She will sing the savageness out of a bear" (4.1.188–89), Iago's "encave yourself" (4.1.81), the storm's "windshak'd surge, with high and monstrous main," which "Seems to cast water on the burning Bear" (2.1.13–14). Shakespeare seemed painfully aware that neighboring the Globe theater wasn't a cathedral but a bear-baiting ring, though it wasn't until *The Winter's Tale* that he actually got one on the stage. Certainly, Othello is more than a bear, and Iago less than a dog (Othello's "Thou hadst been better have been born a dog"; Roderigo's "O inhuman dog"; Lodovico's "O Spartan dog!"). And, if Othello's identification with Iago is as complete as recent readings of the play either demonstrate or assume, who can really say if Othello is a bear or a dog, and it would be a strange scene anyway, a dog set on a dog, a kind of suicide: "I took by th' throat the circumcised dog / And smote him—thus."

So far we have considered the play as an investigation of representation and belief, of jealousy as a metaphor that bridges the two. The other in *Othello*, that which sets itself against the play's preoccupation with representation, with its own status as Othello's life-story, is power, the uses and abuses of power, locally and afar. For there is a conflict in the play—Iago is its focus—between what power represents and what represents power. The general's ancient, or standard-bearer, Iago is literally the sign of a power, a tremendous will to power that is ultimately his own. But, insofar as his power works entirely through, and lives no longer than, the fictions he has fabricated, Iago also sets in motion the forces of representation. An ensign, he ensigns. Shakespeare seems quite generally concerned with the relationship between narrative and power, and we are meant to see the relationship between Othello's jealousy and the affairs of Venice. The First Senator's report of the Turkish bluff toward Rhodes, rather than Cyprus, "'Tis a pageant / To keep us in false gaze," is no doubt intended to suggest a large-scale version of Iago's deception of Othello, and the Senators' reports of the Turkish fleet should probably be read as prefigurative of Othello's mounting jealousy, in a kind of crescendo: "My letters say a hundred and seven galleys"; "And mine a hundred forty"; "And mine two hundred!" (1.3.3–4). The Turkish threat generally is a backdrop for the male rivalry that motivates Iago, and here *Othello*, like other Shakespearean tragedies, domesticates the large-scale violence of brothers spread out across the histories and the Roman plays. Othello suggests his own fraternity with Iago, "And he that is approv'd in this offense, / Though he had twinn'd with me, both at a birth, / Shall lose me" (2.3.211–13), but Shakespeare had already made Iago's motiveless malignity fraternal in *As You Like It*, in which Oliver says of his brother, Orlando: "for my soul (yet I know not why) hates nothing more than he" (1.1.165–66). Fraternal violence is motiveless *because* it is fraternal; "the storied twins," as Fineman notes in a reading of fratricide in *Hamlet*, "thus fight not so much to settle the differences between them (which, of course, can only barely exist, since equivalent brothers fight because they are the 'same'), but instead to establish through violence a definitive difference—victor-vanquished—by means of which they can be distinguished each from each."[3] If the ends of power are arbitrary, or forever beyond the means of power, fratricide is the archetype of all historical violence, at least for Shakespeare. Fineman remarks Shakespeare's willingness to rewrite history, as with Hal and Hotspur, to suggest fraternity where age or circumstance suggested otherwise—that is, when history wouldn't do it for him, as in Antony's marriage to Octavia. Shakespeare wants us to read fraternal rivalry as a subtext for the larger processes of civil war, of history, but in *Othello* a different kind of metaphor surfaces as a model for historical process. Iago is one more Shakespearean brother, but there is a difference between the "leperous distillment" poured by Claudius into the porches of Hamlet's ear and Iago's "I'll pour this pestilence into his ear" (2.3.356). Both plays put forth a specular struggle for power, but *Othello* shows it mediated everywhere by narrative, and narrative mediated everywhere by jealousy, "begot," like the specular struggle it grounds, "upon itself, born of itself" (3.4.162). Whereas the history plays, or Shakespeare's other tragedies, interiorize historical process as narrative, *Othello* reverses this, foregrounding narrative as historical process, acting out the violence of brothers entirely on the level of figure. It is an important question, whether the arbitrary rivalry of twins produces myths as the legitimizing narratives of its own undifferentiated violence (to echo Fineman) or whether such myths, as Titania tells Oberon, "are the forgeries of jealousy" (*Midsummer Night's Dream*, 2.1.81).

Our title has perhaps already suggested that we turn to *Othello* here as a dramatization of this question as it occurs today, in literary theory, between a criticism of power and a criticism of representation, between, very broadly, Marxism and deconstruction. The title also suggests that the work of Frank Lentricchia, particularly as it relates to his reading of Paul de Man, will serve as a focus for this consideration. For in both of Lentricchia's first two works of criticism, *After the New Criticism* (1980) and *Criticism and Social Change* (1983), de Man figures prominently as an extreme instance of representation gone awry, of a radical immersion in the figurative at the expense of history, persuasion, process, and the possibility of social change, this at a time in the United States, and in history, "when everything seems to be flowing the wrong way."[4] For Lentricchia there is nothing ironic about de Man's description of the ironic writer, who, like de Man, "'remains endlessly caught in the impossibility of making [his] knowledge applicable to the empirical world.'"[5] To remain within the properly Shakespearean context adduced by Fineman, and at the same time to move to the second of Lentricchia's books, in de Man's criticism, Lentricchia argues, "forces of differentiation are simply 'torn apart' (de Man's words) by a power that returns literature to radical freedom from all context, except its own literary-historical context, just as Prospero, in the end, permits Ariel's return to unfettered airiness" (63). This "return to unfettered airiness" is also a return, for Lentricchia, to the fin de siècle, art-for-art's-sake aestheticism of an earlier generation of Yale New Critics. What concerns Lentricchia is that such an aesthetic robs criticism of an active engagement with the world, and what bothers him is the way, despite its seeming ineffectualness, de Man's criticism has exerted such a strong and unchallenged influence over his followers. To remain, if not within Shakespeare, within the Italy of lieutenants and their generals, Lentricchia observes how, "in the manner of a don [Don Paolo, *capo di tutti capi*] whose power is assured and unquestioned, de Man has found it necessary to speak only sparingly; in comparison to his prolific lieutenants he is almost invisible" (*After the New Criticism*, 284). I cite this last because it shows up an unresolved paradox at the core of Lentricchia's reading, one whereby de Man is at once the most debilitating and powerful of critics, the most detached and most influential, as if the excessive irony that removes his criticism from the world somehow placed it, still more ironically, tangential and, finally, central. I call this paradox unresolved not merely because Lentricchia never adequately addresses it but because, as we shall see, it is out of this very paradox that his critique of de Man emerges. Simultaneously lamenting de Man's "will to enervation" and his "unquestioned authority," the *irony* of Lentricchia's reading of de Man is that it can never absolutely escape the latter's "powerlessness."

Criticism and Social Change thus picks up, three years later, exactly where *After the New Criticism* leaves off, with an account of the "political paralysis" engendered by de Man's "disjuncture of persuasion and trope." Unlike the first book, however, *Criticism and Social Change* proceeds to offer an alternative to de Man in the work of Kenneth Burke. For Lentricchia there are two problems with de Man's notion of (variously) "pure," "highly synchronic," "utopian," "autonomous" performance: it exiles the intellectual from any unmediated relation with history, and it plays squarely—sheeplike, he will suggest—into the untroubled powers that be. The "problem" with de Man's problem is that his attitude, at once radically unbeholden to and violently in the service of political power, has both nothing and everything to do with history, but this doesn't seem to bother Lentricchia. Nor is he concerned that, at once beyond the margins and the principal theme of such violence, de Man's "radical freedom from all context" represents the extremest instance of what Lentricchia calls a genuinely radical criticism, which "must work its way through capitalism's language of domination by working cunningly within it, using, appropriating, even speaking through its key mechanisms of repression" (24). De Man *absolutely* acquiesces to historical process, since it is motiveless, but, since it is motiveless, undermines its authority *absolutely*. That reading, at least implicitly, is reserved for Burke. Lentricchia's de Man, who is really a kind of straw de Man, overcomes the permanent "disjuncture of persuasion and trope" and comes down firmly on the side of trope and synchrony and purity, when de Man himself has regularly cautioned against such a reading and, more, already worked through the less than purely synchronic assumptions that prompt it. But, so long as de Man makes impossible a certain theoretical investment in social change, everything from Nicaragua to SALT II can be blamed on him, and this explains Lentricchia's tone. Because the political stakes are so high, and because the pervading ideology is so dangerously contentious and puritanical, de Man's ahistoricism is (variously) "perverse," "insidious," "subversive," "scary," even "de-monic." These puritan strains will need to be restruck when we come back to the end of *Othello*.

Enter Kenneth Burke, and I put it this way because that is how Lentricchia puts it, in the book's opening pages, while reconstructing the 1935 American Writers' Congress: "Enter, into this scene of left-wing confidence, Kenneth Burke" (22). Burke's entrance into the first chapter via a stage direction needs to be read against the book's ongoing dramatization of theory, its "intellectual theater" (23), as Lentricchia describes the congress, with what quickly becomes its almost psychomachian struggle between the forces of darkness and light for the soul of the American intellectual. Hence the de-monic de Man but also, and perhaps more urgently, the closing chapter's "I have been tempted to offer Burke as the angel of modern criticism" (158). For, even if Burke and de Man "are not . . . allegorical pictures of good and evil" (20), Lentricchia clearly opts for good, and the book ends with the comic (*because* divinely sanctioned) marriage of heaven and hell, narrative and history. Lentricchia recalls Burke's early and mistaken dismissal of the effects of historical process on the loftier spirit as "the Calibanization of Ariel," but this also names Lentricchia's revision, through Burke, of de Man, who two pages later is likened to Ariel. The comic genre of "Calibanization"—a process that can be referred back to Fineman as a moment when the shaping influence of Shakespearean language, and the Shakespearean subject, surfaces in contemporary criticism—bears noting because it is against comedy that the book is written, the genre of Lentricchia's de Man and the early Burke, whose work proceeds "from a vantage point beyond [history's] conflicts: the critic as comedic master takes the place of God" (64). The problem, then, with Lentricchia's "angel-of-modern-criticism" happy ending is that committed political action triumphs over rhetorical undecidability, but the happy ending is a triumph for narrative, with this difference: narrative returns to Lentricchia's valorization of

Burke even as it returns to de Man's dismissal of history, but its return in *Criticism and Social Change* is no longer merely comic, since the narrative in question tells the triumph of history. In *Criticism and Social Change* there are two narratives, one comic and one no longer comic, the Calibanization of Ariel but just where it turns to, say, the "cannibalization" of Lear. Lentricchia's Burke differs from Lentricchia's de Man not as history differs from narrative but, from within narrative, as comedy differs from tragedy.

What the entrance of theater itself into theory signals is a moment of transference in which the subject of literature becomes a subject of interpretation. The subject of *Criticism and Social Change* is a divided one, and divided not just between Burke and de Man or between these two and Lentricchia, but between history and narrative, and theater and theory. What Burke and de Man represent for Lentricchia are the mutually exclusive origins of his own critical orientation, origins that, self-canceling and therefore ungrounded as they are, are themselves at the origin of the book's recourse to theater, "with Burke enacting the father's role of historical materialist" (23) as against de Man's predicted future for critical theory, "in effect, the miming of himself as critical father" (39). What these mirroring fathers represent, mythic but only because they are mirroring, is the space of Lentricchia's subject, who is also Burke's subject, and a divided one: "The 'present' that Burke defines is nothing but the intersection of past and future. . . . What Burke in *Counter Statement* calls the 'contemporary,' or the artist's 'situation,' is the 'present,' of course, but a present not present to itself" (118; Fineman's "The subject of Shakespeare's sonnets experiences himself *as* his difference from himself" [25]). If the book's greatest virtue is that some mechanism of self-differentiation is working effectively enough to generate a subject of real interest and controversy, the effect is a spiraling one, a call to action already worked by a kind of acting, which, realized, requires a stronger calling, which produces more theater. Lentricchia describes this process when he quotes Burke's discussion of the expression "the motivation of an act," wherein, Burke says, "we may discern a dramatistic pun":

> To consider an *act* in terms of its *grounds* is to consider it in terms of what it is not, namely, in terms of motives that, in acting upon the active, would make it passive. We could state the paradox another way by saying that the concept of activation implies a kind of passive-behind-the-passive; for an agent

who is "motivated by his passions" would be "moved by his being-movedness" or "acted upon by his state of being acted upon." (73)

Here is the de Manian *mise-en-abyme* so feared by Lentricchia, an infinite regress of "act" perpetually trumped by a motivation that makes action passive, and passive (somehow) *because* motiveless, but this contradiction is no longer

> the despair of history. Rather, it is first the very condition of transformation that makes a certain kind of historical consciousness possible; second, it is the condition that opens, once and for all, the autonomous, closed, and unified subject to historical process; Burke deconstructs the subject *in order to* historicize it. (75)

The "unresolvable ambiguity" of *act* situates Lentricchia's subject in the space of "a strange self-difference" within action, which is Lentricchia's reading of de Man but is here his reading of Burke. The difference Burke adds to de Man is history, even if this difference is— if only historically—made by de Man. Lentricchia's subject is suspended between these two alternatives, between an active (motivated) Burke and a Burke already answered by a passive-behind-the-passive de Man, but the book never addresses the paradox it was written to solve, that de Man's "powerlessness" has somehow shown itself far more influential than Burke's "engagement." Lentricchia finds in Burke's reading of *act* a Burke radically different from himself, but, because everything in the book points to de Man as this radical other, the more unlike Burke Burke becomes, the more like de Man he is, so that his difference from himself is always a function (for Lentricchia) of his difference from de Man—"What he [Burke] has done to 'act' (another foreshadowing, with a difference, of de Man) . . ." (74). Between worlds politically and theatrically "acted upon," Lentricchia's Burke is divided from an idealist tradition by an other who is insistently, if silently, the same, until the right-wing acquiescence Lentricchia somewhat absurdly reads into de Man's deconstruction of motive gives way to a subject somehow wholly contrary, but really only all the more committed to the same traditionalist ideology it *invents,* a subject somehow alien to a certain "Republican" passivity Lentricchia loosely associates with de Man and the Yale criticism of the 1980s but really all the more right, all the more fanatically puritanical, all the more precariously poised on the extremest margins of potential and explosive action, even, if possible, all the more theatrical. Enter "the Dirty Harry of contemporary critical theory," as Lentricchia is referred to on the back of the paperback edition of *Criticism and Social Change.*

Returning to *Othello*, it may be useful to consider the nature of Lentricchia's disagreement with de Man in light of the play—for example, the way *Criticism and Social Change* begins where the play does, with a chapter called "Provocations." "Tush, never tell me," Roderigo tells Iago in the play's opening line, but the book begins "I can tell you what my book is about, at its polemical core." Like Iago—it will be clearer that this comparison with Iago is not intended to be critical, in the first place because, as we shall see, there is more than one Iago in the Lentricchia–de Man controversy, in the second because it is the limits of the "critical" itself that will need to be considered, and in the third because Lentricchia's final position, borrowed from Kenneth Burke, not only sounds like de Man but would seem to offer a valuable insight into the play's investigation of power and representation: "Burke . . . raises the aesthetic to the decisive sphere of hegemonic function where the war over the political formation of consciousness is fought out" (101)—like Iago, then, what ticks Lentricchia off is that a "bookish theoric," Cassio, has been promoted over him, or rather over Kenneth Burke, whom Lentricchia nicely holds up as the antithesis of de Man. "'Mere repetition, mere fiction and allegory, forever unable to participate in the spontaneity of action and modernity,'" Lentricchia notes of de Man (48); "Mere prattle without practice," Iago says (1.1.26).[6] The provocations past, the protagonists are introduced. "My cast is very small," Lentricchia tells us. "Its main actors are Kenneth Burke and Paul de Man" (19). Twinned at a birth, they grow to find themselves at roughly opposite ends of the critical spectrum: "One of the great things about Burke is that he knew the truths of de Man early, and he knew them without the disastrous political effects that seem everywhere to track de Man and his students." There is a problem, Lentricchia feels, with the inevitable de Manian notion of textual blockage, which ultimately leads—this is the dominant theme of his reading of de Man—to paralysis, "'Paralyzed force, gesture without motion'" (51). Othello falls into a trance, Iago above him:

Work on.
My med'cine works! Thus credulous fools are caught,

And many worthy and chaste dames even thus
(All guiltless) meet reproach. What, ho! My lord!
My lord, I say! Othello!

(4.1.44–48)

Othello, like de Man, is paralyzed by a fiction, a representational
realm so pure that actual poisons, "Not poppy nor mandragora," Iago
says in an aside, "Shall ever medicine thee to that sweet sleep / Which
thou ow'dst yesterday" (3.3.330–33). This is de Man as Othello, with
Kenneth Burke, for the sake of symmetry, as Iago. But when Iago says,
"Dangerous conceits are in their natures poisons" (3.3.326), this
reduction of the physical to the figurative is de Man, too. One senses
that Lentricchia is trying very hard to keep de Man in Othello's position, but when Iago paralyzes Othello with a representation this is de
Man at both extremes. For his part Burke himself has argued for "the
ultimate interchangeability of Othello and Iago,"[7] though in an essay
admittedly from the period before his supposed falling off with de Man
and at a time in the history of *Othello* scholarship (1951) when no less
than three essays were published asserting, in one form or another,
that Iago represents something already in Othello. Lentricchia is both-
ered above all by "the wholly interiorized self of de Man's analysis"
(42), which he sets against Burke's "historical and cultural specificity"
(33), but, as Burke says, "the very extremity of inwardness in the
motives of Iago can make it seem an outwardness . . . Villain and hero
here are essentially parts of the one fascination" (166). Thus, what
Lentricchia ultimately comes to realize, or seems to realize, is that the
split Burke makes with de Man never occurred, never could occur,
that history and power are already worked by the wholly interiorized
space of a de Manian representation. It is a pivotal moment in the
story, his story, Lentricchia tells us, when the narrative he has set
against the "insidious effect" of de Man's comes to recognize it is
toward that very representation that its movement has been directed.
It is a pivotal moment in the story because it is here that what Lentricchia is doing becomes a story, for him—here that we find, he says, "a
de Man in us all." Lest we overlook all that is at stake here, Lentricchia even gives his story a genre, but our running comparison with
Othello leaves little doubt of that:

> There is a de Man in us all. For similar unsettling reasons, like
> Borges he is one of our representative men. One of the great
> things about Burke is that he knew the truths of de Man early,
> and he knew them without the disastrous political conse-

quences that seem everywhere to track de Man and his students. The subject belongs to Henry James: there is a moment in "The Jolly Corner," a pivotal moment for that story, and for mine, in which one of James's characters broods over the question of his inaction. And the brooding turns quickly into agony over the awareness that the paralysis of inaction is doubled in the consciousness of such. "Oh to have this consciousness was to *think*—and to think . . . as he stood there, was, with the lapsing moments, not to have acted! Not to have acted—that was the misery and the pang—was even still not to act; was in fact *all* to feel the thing in another, in a new and terrible way."

"Yes," Lentricchia adds, "but 'The Jolly Corner' has a happy ending" (51).

F. R. Leavis, in one of the essays from 1951–52, notes how "Iago's power . . . is that he represents something that is in Othello . . . the essential traitor is within the gates."[8] Leavis cuts across the alternatives of power and representation ("Iago's power . . . is that he represents") just as the metaphor of insurrection he attaches joins imagination and the state, reminding us that the oppositions Lentricchia's reading depends on—de Man/Burke, deconstruction/Marxism, interior/exterior, representation/history—rework the microcosm-macrocosm relation that governs all Renaissance appropriations of the domestic by the historical. Lentricchia cuts across similar alternatives when he says "the insidious effect of his [de Man's] work is . . . the paralysis of praxis itself" (40). For we are not meant to take lightly Lentricchia's "there is a de Man in us all." In context it is a monumental assertion, one de Man would probably take as the crux of Lentricchia's entire reading, but so might Lentricchia; given the utterance, he already has, if de Man has. One senses, perhaps incorrectly, that Lentricchia reads Burke as a de Man who wised up because, in thinking through their relation, Lentricchia came to find Burke more and more taken up with the very themes, and the very moves, that inflict de Man. For the narrative of their falling out may be, as such narratives often are, the response to a persistent and surprising falling in, as if Lentricchia himself were a de Manian but the first to feel what he laments none of de Man's followers feel, an "anxiety of influence" (39). His retrospective priority to de Man through Burke would be Bloom's model. I say this by way of moving toward this same moment in Othello's story, where it is also tinged with anxiety, and pivotal, because it is here that Othello turns, here that he first gives way to the jealousy that will consume him. What makes the moment so unusual, and, again, pivotal, is that the words that drive him into fits of suspicion are his own:

> *Iago:* Indeed!
> *Othello:* Indeed? Ay, indeed! Discern'st thou aught in that?
>   Is he not honest?
> *Iago:*   Honest, my lord?
> *Othello:* Honest? Ay, honest.
> *Iago:*   My lord, for aught I know.
>
> *Othello:* What dost thou think?
> *Iago:*   Think my lord?
> *Othello:* Think, my lord? By heaven, thou echoest me,
>   As if there were some monster in thy thought
>   Too hideous to be shown.
>
>   (3.3.101–8)

It is important to remember that Iago first works Othello into a pitch not by suggesting Desdemona's adultery but by refusing to suggest anything. I think the Lentricchia–Othello–de Man scenario has played its course, but one can still note that, amazingly, what bothers Lentricchia is that de Man "has nothing to say" (40). It would take some doing to show that the perpetual intersection of history and representation is thought, but this is what Iago repeats, Othello's thought, by refusing to reveal his own. The next time we see them together, act 4, scene 1, finds them entering in mid-conversation, but by now the echo has repeated itself to the point of infinite reversal:

> *Iago:* Will you think so?
> *Othello:*   Think so, Iago?
>
>   (4.1.1–2)

When the general confronts his ancient, power confronts its symbol, history confronts representation. Neither side prevails, since the undoing of power by trope constitutes an interminable regression, and one therefore properly "motiveless" in the very different senses used by Coleridge (Iago's "motiveless malignity") and de Man; one side just gets tired of waiting. Sixty lines separate "By heaven, thou echoest me" from "By heaven, I'll know thy thoughts," but Othello is no closer, for Iago can wait a long time, forever, he tells Othello. When Lentricchia notes in *After the New Criticism* that "de Man fudges" (315), delay, the waiting game, was already the crux of his complaint.

In the closing pages of *Criticism and Social Change,* when the *how* of genuine social change will no longer be put off, Lentricchia's last resort is to the original return of narrative in history, to myth:

> Burke encapsulates his theory of poetic expression . . . by appealing to the story of Perseus and Medusa, a myth more central to poetics, from his point of view, than the story of Orpheus and his voyage to Hades: "Perseus, who could not face the serpent-headed monster without being turned to stone, but was immune to this danger if he observed it to be a reflection in a mirror." The mirror [of socially effective literature] does what Burke insists representation cannot help doing—it represents with a difference; it bears purpose; it is itself an act of power in that it controls the murderous Medusa and, performing this initial act, prepares for another: the decapitation of the Medusa. (156)

Here the Shakespearean mirror would more literally resemble the one that Richard II shatters at the moment of his deposition. For it is this mirror that the earl of Essex, in best Persean mode, holds up to Elizabeth on the eve of his failed rebellion, a mirror in which Elizabeth also saw herself, so that the deposition scene was never published in her lifetime. Richard's mirror shows him his own image reversed, the second Richard he has always been, but what it shows Elizabeth is the dangerously close rhetorical and historical aporia of a self-styled "poet-king." Macbeth looks in a very different mirror from Richard's and holds it up to James in a way that confirms rather than threatens his rule, unfolding the legitimate line of Banquo extended even to James. Macbeth's mirror will confirm "to th' crack of doom," he believes. For the line established by the play begins from *his* decapitation, or from his "decapitation" of Duncan, which ends the previous line (Macduff's "destroy your sight / With a new Gorgon" [2.3.71– 72]).[9] The evanescence of even the surest scenario, with respect to the mirror of narrative's relation to history, is a danger not just for narrative, least of all narratives like Lentricchia's or Macbeth's. It was, of course, not Elizabeth but Macbeth, Richard, Essex, and James's *son* who were beheaded. Whereas Elizabeth sees herself in Richard's mirror, Macbeth sees James in his, and this cross-coupling of theater and power, into the mirror and out from it, is the mirror that the Shakespearean subject holds up to history, and to *Criticism and Social*

Change. In the book's fourth chapter Samuel Johnson's ambivalence toward Shakespeare "becomes a mirror of social change" (136). Lentricchia's double and doubly returning subject, a subject divided from him- or herself, first and foremost, before all the interminable declensions of psychology, by history's difference from narrative, could be shown in other ways, but the presence of Shakespearean language in Lentricchia's book, particularly through Burke, makes the Shakespearean subject especially pertinent to Lentricchia's account of the "political aesthetic." What the politics of his reading finesse is the way his engagement with history is perpetually mediated—this is not just the moral but the fact of the Perseus myth—by representation, and representation represented in a mirror. Lentricchia's struggle with history is a function, first, of his struggle with this mirror, especially because, given the book's project of an unmediated opening of narrative onto history, the mirror he strikes by is the one he must shatter, and shatter *in order to* strike. This is roughly his position vis-à-vis de Man. There can be perhaps no more revolutionary *act* than the demonstration that history itself is subject, somewhere and by definition, to rhetorical imperatives, for only then can figure be subjected, systematically but also spontaneously, to historical change. Lentricchia understands this; it is part of "the maximal claim," he believes, but, instead of using this insight to advance a socially viable reading of rhetorical responsibility, he takes on the insight. The result of this resistance is a series of actions that confine themselves to the sphere of criticism and not social change. It is the presence of de Man that precludes motivated political action, the book argues, and proves. But only because it is also the presence of de Man that makes such action possible—so long, that is, as such action is taken (understood and effected) rhetorically, within the properly critical space of narrative's relation to power. The book proves this, too: however "new" the historicism (or the Gorgon), it will be old—that is, find itself historically consigned not just to the limits of narrative but of theory too—the moment it works against rather than within de Man's deconstruction of motive. Nor will it be able to proceed beyond, as a number of recent readings attest, the perpetual undoing of this same deconstruction. It is doubtful that Lentricchia's book, for all its bravado, has touched off any decapitations, and, while Lentricchia finds himself reflected in Perseus, the Medusa mirrored in his book is, again, not history but de Man (the Medusean paranoia, of course, but only because the same *paralysis*).[10]

I want to conclude by turning very briefly to Stephen Greenblatt's essay "The Improvisation of Power," a valuable reading of *Othello* that ends his book *Renaissance Self-Fashioning.* Greenblatt finds in *Othello* "the supreme symbolic expression" of a certain cultural mode, one of willful submission to fictions in the service of a power; for Iago improvisation "is the key to a mastery whose emblem is the 'duteous and knee-crooking knave' who dotes 'on his own obsequious bondage' (1.1.145–46), a mastery invisible to the servant, a mastery, that is, whose character is essentially ideological."[11] So pervasive is the consuming power of narrative in the play that it runs, like Othello's life-story, " 'To the very moment that he bade me tell it.' We are on the brink," Greenblatt continues, "of a Borges-like narrative of the present instant, a narrative in which the story teller is constantly swallowed up by the story" (238). Naturally, this would extend to Greenblatt's retelling too; as noted earlier, we are meant to hear the echo of his own name in an allusion to jealousy and its relation to the beginnings of Shakespearean criticism: "To an envious contemporary like Robert Greene, Shakespeare seems a kind of green-room Iago, appropriating for himself the labor of others. . . . Still, at the least we must grant . . . that it would have seemed fatal to be imitated by Shakespeare. He possessed a limitless talent for entering into the consciousness of another, perceiving its deepest structures as a manipulable fiction, reinscribing it into his own narrative form" (252). The chapter merges two readings of improvisation, as power and as representation. Iago celebrates the insinuating rhetoric of colonialism and the wholesale religious conversions that depend on it, as if, one might infer, the national theater were performing the same function in the colonization of England itself. A play that lays bare the evils of such a process is only partially an apology for it, and even Iago, for all he capitalizes on, is a reluctant capitalist. His refrainlike advice to Roderigo, "Put money in thy purse," is a lip-service tribute to the ballooning GNP from one who, "belee'd and calm'd / By debitor and creditor" (1.1.30–31), despairs that "Preferment goes by letter and affection, / And not by old gradation" (36–37). On the other hand, who's going to believe Iago? Or Shakespeare, for that matter? As Greenblatt notes, "Shakespeare's language and themes are caught up, like the medium itself, in unsettling repetitions, committed to the shifting voices and audiences, with their shifting aesthetic assumptions and historical imperatives, that govern a living theater" (254).

This is where the chapter ends (save a fine one-paragraph tribute to Desdemona), but the book ends with an epilogue, the brief account of a plane flight from Baltimore to Boston, on which Greenblatt has just settled down to a rereading of Clifford Geertz's *Interpretation of Cultures.* A middle-aged man is beside him, en route to his son in a

Boston hospital whom a disease, among other effects, has rendered speechless. Greenblatt is asked if he would "mime a few sentences so that he could practice reading my lips? Would I say, soundlessly, 'I want to die. I want to die'?" (255). Greenblatt, politely enough, tells him to go "practice on himself in front of a mirror." "It's not the same," the man replies. Greenblatt refuses; who wouldn't? "To abandon self-fashioning . . . is to die"—to repeat the man's phrase is to submit to its meaning, to want to die. "Paranoia tinged my whole response. . . . I felt superstitiously that if I mimed the man's terrible sentence, it would have the force, as it were, of a legal sentence" (256). The mime, the disease, the speechlessness, even the lips are *Othello*, but the repeated phrase is Freud, the insoluble linking of death instinct and repetition compulsion. For Greenblatt the man is a threat ("I was afraid that he was, quite simply, a maniac"), as if the man, say, offended by Greenblatt's casual rereading of *The Interpretation of Cultures* while he, his fellow passenger, perhaps already terrified of flying, can't even take off his seatbelt and get a *Sports Illustrated,* and would not do so if he could, being inclined to conversation, or to cards, had grabbed Greenblatt's collar as the plane banked north and screamed, "Oh yeah, mime 'I want to die' so I can read your lips!" Hey, it could happen.

Driving off the lot, I look in the rearview mirror. Iago.

Synchronic Theory and
Absolutism: *"Et tu, Brute?"*

Antony and Cleopatra offers a useful reference for an important debate surrounding the work of Paul de Man. In the decade preceding the discovery of de Man's wartime journalism, a number of critics had already referred to a tacit but deep conservatism in his "Hamlet-like ironic detachment from the world of practical affairs; for such readers de Man's radical reduction of history and psychology to "truth's inability to coincide with itself," to an aporia inherent in representation, neutralizes from the beginning any possibility for motivated political action.[1] Marx, of course, had made similar claims in *The German Ideology* regarding the Young Hegelians, and, much more recently, critics such as John Fekete had written related and influential critiques of American New Criticism, substituting "agrarianism" for the "idealism" attacked by Marx, and for what would later become the "quietism" associated with de Man.[2] The principal source for this reading of de Man, however, is Adorno, whose work is regularly concerned with detailing the deep investment of ahistoric theory in the totalizing powers it claims to obviate or undo. In the terms of this debate, the de Man of trope and Nietzschean forgetting is the de Man of imperative and Nietzschean power; in the terms of the play, Egypt is Rome—or, rather, the more Egypt, the more Rome.

This is a reasonable thesis, and one Shakespeare seems to share. The play works like a grand deconstruction of the two worlds, and, if Caesar rules Rome like a logos, Cleopatra governs Egypt according to all the deconstructive paradoxes—"makes hungry / Where most she satisfies" (2.2.236–37), "and what they undid did" (205), "bless her when she is riggish" (239), and so on. Without suggesting that *différance* represents the punning Cleopatra for which an entire school of American literary theory has given the world, it is worth emphasizing that all the Shakespearean paradoxes that "make defect perfection" (2.2.231) in Cleopatra represent for the play a similar deconstructive noncenter, but one that has itself been deeply politicized. "It goes without saying that it cannot be *exposed*," Derrida remarks of *différance*, but gone is the extraordinary class metaphor of Enobarbus's "For her own person, / It beggar'd all description" (2.2.197–98).[3] Such juxtapositions might suggest that the terms of contemporary literary theory closely parallel those of Shakespearean drama, but what the comparison really suggests is that the plays themselves are already scenes of interpretation whose subject, as we will determine, is their own relation to power. In this they most resemble the literary theory to which they will be referred here, increasingly powerful figurations of a progressive internalization of figure's own relation to power. Thus, in Saussure's almost revolutionary conclusion that "in language there are only differences *without positive terms*," there are, strictly speaking, nine positive terms.[4] If the words are true they are not even there, and if they are false they are true, since it is precisely this disappearance of any truth content, or signified, that creates the purely differential play, in this case, of nine positive terms. Signification is finally signified, but only because it is performed or enacted rather than paraphrased or interpreted, even as the italics underscoring *"without positive terms,"* highlighting the three "positive terms," are ironic, theory *as* theater. When, on the other hand, Saussure suggests in the same summational paragraph that "the idea or the phonic substance that a sign contains is of less importance than the other signs that surround it," this, too, is an idea, the idea that "the idea or the phonic substance that a sign contains is of less importance than the other signs that surround it." As such, the sentence cannot be removed from its immediate context without losing its significance, but few sentences from Saussure's *Course in General Linguistics* are more frequently cited.

With additional reference, then, to the anagrammatic intersection of Saussure and Rousseau in a somehow *post*-Saussurean study like Derrida's *Of Grammatology*, we need to consider in a little more detail the precise relation of synchronic theory to absolutism. The earliest essay to juxtapose on a large scale synchronic linguistics and literary theory was Roman Jakobson's "Linguistics and Poetics." The essay, first delivered at Indiana University in 1958, exerted a strong influence on de Man, for whom "contemporary literary theory comes into its own in such events as the application of Saussurean linguistics to literary texts."[5] Whereas Saussure had developed a model for synchronic linguistics, Jakobson's goal in the essay is to translate that model into a "synchronic poetics."[6] I do not want to rehearse his argument here but move directly to his concluding example. This is a careful grammatical and lexical unfolding of Antony's funeral oration for Caesar in *Julius Caesar*, which Jakobson condenses to the following:

> The noble Brutus
> Hath told you Caesar was ambitious . . .
> For Brutus is an honorable man . . .
> But Brutus says he was ambitious,
> And Brutus is an honorable man . . .
> Yet Brutus says he was ambitious,
> And Brutus is an honorable man . . .
> Yet Brutus says he was ambitious,
> And, sure, he is an honorable man.

Jakobson emphasizes the way grammar functions to convey irony, turning reported facts into reported speech. Our concern now is not with the correctness of his grammatical method—de Man himself takes this up in "Semiology and Rhetoric"—but, rather, to follow in a little more detail the relation of synchronic theory and absolutism implicit in the *selection* of this passage and not another. The essay's more famous "I like Ike" example is a primitive enough assertion of support for the status quo, but one that suspends identification between resemblance (*I* sounds like *Ike*) and desire, between an authority in the world and the seemingly separate authority of a language that makes *Ike* like *I*—and, more powerfully, *like* like *like*. The essay as a transitional mode between synchronic linguistics and synchronic poetics is useful for the way it suggests the necessarily complex relation of both to historical process and to related questions of influence and tradition. When, early in the essay, Jakobson illustrates the metalingual function of language with "'I don't follow you—what do you mean?' . . . or in Shakespearean diction, 'What is't thou say'st?'" (93), he labors the point but only to bring in the Shakespearean context that Antony will ultimately bring to fruition. When, even earlier, he illustrates what he calls the phatic function with "'Are you listening?' or in Shakespearean diction, 'Lend me your ears'" (92), he is not only borrowing directly from the oration but setting up a relation to his audience modeled explicitly on Antony's relation to his. Of course, even given his first name, Roman, the Jakobson of "Linguistics and Poetics" is not exclusively Antony, or Brutus, for that matter, "the noblest Roman of them all." Nor has he come to bury Saussure, but to praise him. On the other hand, a juxtaposition of proper names—in which Saussure himself attempted to inscribe the subject of Latin poetry from within synchrony—suggests how, in this particular roman à clef (and antonomasia), a succession from Caesar to Antony is being laid over a succession from Saussure to Roman Jakobson. In the essay's closing remarks the two subjects converge, the synchronic theorist and the Roman (and ultimately Jacobean) hero, just at the moment when identity itself is conferred:

> My attempt to vindicate the right and duty of linguistics to direct the investigation of verbal art in all its compass and extent can come to a conclusion with the same burden which summarized my report to the 1953 conference here at Indiana University: *"Linguista sum: linguistici nihil a me alienum puto."* (120)

Saussure is vindicated, but in the language of Antony—or Caesar, we may assume, given Jakobson's earlier "the symmetry of the three disyllabic verbs with an identical initial consonant and identical final vowel added splendor to the laconic victory message of Caesar: *'Veni, vidi, vici'"* (96). The essay ends by making explicit, and explicitly personal, the synchronic dispersal of historical power in a pattern of images that underwrites the essay's claims to, if not "vindication," succession.

These are preliminary remarks that may guide us as we turn now directly to de Man's wartime writings. What makes these writings so important is that they bring to the surface the complicit relation to established power—and to an absolutist ideology—that his later work had already been said to repress or hide or excuse or allegorize but always draw on. "Absolutism" will name here an authority that, answering only to itself, rules *by* the power it rules *with*, a performative-constative difference developed most fully by de Man in his reading of autobiography, a genre that shares the textual logic of absolutism (as Hitler's *Mein Kampf* or Caesar's *Bellum Gallicum* might suggest).[7] It is this difference that every mandate or imperative seeks to close but necessarily deepens, occasioning a stronger imperative. Absolutism in this sense is absolute not because it reaches everywhere but because it can't stop. Or start. It can't stop because it can't start—this we will refer to as its properly *historical* power.

The questions raised by de Man's early association with this imperative, however one understands it, are deeply complicated. This is in part by reason of his own biography, by his commitment to Flemish autonomy, and by the no doubt powerful influence of his uncle Henri de Man. The association with absolutism is also complicated by the writings themselves. In their most extended discussion of the subject, the report of a lecture at the Institute of Italian Culture entitled "Les systèmes impériaux de la Rome antique" (13 March 1941), de Man follows the editorial line when he notes how modern Italy impressively combines the Romes of Caesar and Augustus, but here and elsewhere it is never clear if this is the lecturer's opinion or de Man's. Nor is this the only opinion. In his article four days later on a second lecture entitled "Le 'Risorgimento' italien" (17 March 1941) the moral drawn from the resurgence of Rome almost seems to step dangerously across that same editorial line: "Et la leçon est importante pour les Belges qui désirent voir leur pays se reconstruire: ils verront comment il faut trouver ses forces régénératrices, non pas en regardant au delà des frontières, mais en tirant parti de qualités spécifiques qui s'étalent tout au long de l'histoire du pays."

No text, of course, joins de Man's early writings to the later work, and no reading can ever ultimately develop their moments of connection, or disprove them. One of the meanings of absolute power for theory may be that its relation to the figural can never be more than felt, nor merely felt in readings like de Man's that develop the absolute power of figure. I want to suggest now: (1) that a thoroughly synchronic theory can only begin by inscribing the unmediated relation to authority played out, in Jakobson's essay, at the level of the proper name (and coextensive, however complicated their complicity, with de Man's wartime writings); and (2) that it can move forward (or constitute a movement) only with reference to an end that is no longer historically absolute but, by contrast, absolutely historical. This last is more than a tautology, as if the end of theory were praxis. In the first place theory, as de Man represents it, "never quite reaches its mark" (*AR*, 130). Nor is the relation of early to late as specular or circular as the previous juxtaposition of terms might suggest. The opposition *late-early* may be undermined in de Man's later writings, but we will see that it is only because the end of theory is perpetually undermined by something like a founding relation to power that it becomes "impossible to decide . . . whether [its] flourishing is a triumph or a fall" (*RT*, 20).

The return of the wartime writings *in* the later work is explicitly at issue in de Man's essay "Excuses"—at least if we are to take seriously its opening footnote to Michel Leiris's "De la littérature considerée comme une tauromachie," to which de Man attaches "The essay dates from 1945, immediately after the war" (*AR*, 278). The reference is perhaps too arbitrary for anything beyond de Man's own wartime writings to really explain it, but it is also autobiographical by default, since de Man praises Leiris's essay because it appears in "a text that is indeed as political as it is autobiographical" (and here de Man attaches the note). So framed, even indited, "Excuses" is autobiographical because it never pretended to be, sentencing de Man for the same failure to reveal that it uncovers in Rousseau, for keeping what he gives away, the exposure of a desire to expose. The essay ends the second part of *Allegories of Reading* on just these terms, reserving its harshest judgment ("what is truly shameful") for what may be its own worst crime, that the slander of the innocent Marion was committed "not for the sake of Rousseau's saving face, nor for the sake of his desire for her, but merely in order . . . to furnish him with a good ending for Book II of his *Confessions*" (286). Viewed against the wartime writings (and "Confiteor" is the last chapter of Henri de Man's autobiography *Après coup*), "Excuses" develops its own "implicit shift from reported guilt to the guilt of reporting" (290), setting in motion the repetition compulsion it describes, and which Freud in fact first notes in cases of war trauma.[8] What makes the essay transitional to work after *Allegories of Reading* is that it thereby interiorizes the very relation to responsibility it continues to undermine, at which point, we will need to consider, its power to undermine is virtually limitless.

In his essay "Rhetoric of Tropes," and again in "Anthropomorphism and Trope in the Lyric," de Man develops a specific but crucial convergence of figure and power when he considers Nietzsche's influential definition of truth as "a mobile army of metaphors" (*ein bewegliches Heer von Metaphern*). In the earlier essay Nietzsche's definition serves to underscore the figural displacement of philosophical "truth"; in the later essay de Man develops the metaphor itself:

> Truth, says Nietzsche, is a mobile *army* of tropes. Mobility is coextensive with any trope, but the connotations introduced by "army" are not so obvious, for to say that truth is an army (of tropes) is again to say something odd and possibly misleading. It can certainly not imply, in *On Truth and Lie*, that truth is a kind of commander who enlists tropes in the battle against error.[9]

The wit of the last sentence is the pun on *enlists troops:* truth is a trope, but de Man's own rhetoric suggests that a trope is a troop. It also makes a trope (paronomasia) of *tropes*, which is no longer the power described by the pun but an image of the power it describes by—the way Nietzsche's "army of metaphors" is no longer a metaphor the moment it becomes a kind of standard for the avant-garde. *Tropes* marks a momentary convergence of performance and paraphrase, a momentary troping of trope, but the same relation is increasingly at issue in de Man's later writing. This can be seen most easily by juxtaposing a relatively early essay like "Literary History and Literary Modernity," in which a troop is unabashedly a trope, with a later essay like "The Resistance to Theory."[10] In the earlier essay de Man considers how, "the more radical the rejection of anything that came before, the greater the dependence on the past" (*BI*, 161); in "The Resistance to Theory" the same dialectic has been internalized, and "the more [literary theory] is resisted, the more it flourishes, since the language it speaks is the language of self-resistance" (19–20). In the earlier essay "literature, which is inconceivable without a passion for modernity, also seems to oppose *from the inside* a subtle resistance to this passion" (154; italics added); in the second essay "theory *is* itself this resistance" (19). Most of the terms are the same from one essay to the other, but the background has shifted. Thus, while Keats's poem "The Fall of Hyperion" serves as an image of the theorist in "Literary History and Literary Modernity" (149), in the later essay it appears instead as an image of theory (16). The earlier essay develops the way literature opposes the very passion for modernity it exemplifies; in "The Resistance to Theory" the same dynamic operates with respect to the essay itself, with respect to theory. The power to which the later essay refers is absolute power but only because that power is, strictly speaking, its own.

For just this reason, however, it may still be the case that the self-determination of figure's relation to power responds just as radically to an absolutist agenda equally its own. In Jakobson's "Linguistics and Poetics" Shakespeare mediates between the universalizing claims of synchronic theory and the absolutism represented by Caesar, and it may be useful to develop this relation more carefully now from within Shakespeare. If *Antony and Cleopatra* (1607) stages the civil war, and the rise of Caesar, that followed events portrayed in *Julius Caesar* (1599), so, in their own ways, do the intervening tragedies. This is especially true in *Hamlet*, where the ghost of Old Hamlet is, again, explicitly a theatrical echo of Caesar's ghost in *Julius Caesar* ("Hic et ubique?" [1.5.156]), and where Hamlet dies against Horatio's "I am more an antique Roman than a Dane" (5.2.341). Macbeth himself draws the comparison to Antony when he says of Banquo, "under him / My Genius is rebuk'd, as it is said / Mark Antony's was by Caesar" (3.1.54–56). At the end of *Othello*, to cite one last example, "Cassio rules in Cyprus" (5.2.332), "a soldier," Iago observes early in the play, "fit to stand by Caesar / And give direction" (2.3.122–23). In these terms each of the major tragedies represents a resistance to the coming order of Caesar on which they end, one by one and as a group.[11]

The relation of figure to power is no doubt as problematic in theater as it is in theory, and I want to consider for a moment only one aspect of its functioning in *Antony and Cleopatra* but one with important—if still unresolved—implications for literary theory. This is the relation of the dialectic to sexual difference. When Cleopatra, reflecting on Antony in a famous passage, remarks how "I drunk him to his bed; / Then put my tires and mantles on him, whilst / I wore his sword Philippan" (2.4.21–23), the surrendering of the sword turns Antony into Cleopatra, but it also turns history—in this case, the ghosting of Brutus at Philippi—into theater. The association is momentary, but the later "boying" of Cleopatra's "greatness" establishes it for the entire play. Both references suggest that figure's difference from history is sexual difference, but they also imply that the more sexual difference is undermined by figure, the closer to a thoroughly historical imperative the representation. To the extent that it coins the word *in order to* crown the king, if *Macbeth* precedes *Antony and Cleopatra* because its drive to *unsex* sexual difference in the Witches' "none of woman born / Shall harm Macbeth" (4.1.80–81) speaks directly to the Caesarean Macduff, "untimely ripp'd" from his mother's womb, *Coriolanus* follows because the hero's mother, Volumnia, *is*, in a very real sense, Rome.

In each of these plays the figure-power dialectic is pushed to its absolute limit, but I want to suggest that the relation of the dialectic itself to sexual difference is, in every case, the same: as long as the title character (or characters, in the relevant case of *Antony and Cleopatra*) remains the locus of unstable gender identifications, the struggle for historical power that a given play chronicles is, again, its own. "Caesar's will?" Cleopatra demands of an incoming messenger (3.13.46), and one doesn't need to be Shakespeare to read through this to "Caesar is Will," or "Will is Caesar's." At the least it must be referred back to the clamor for "Caesar's will" in *Julius Caesar*, which Antony reads to the citizens among a chorus of *will's, well's,* and *we'll's.* This in turn can be referred back to the extended play on *will* in sonnets 135–36. Whether or not "Caesar's will" actually *names* Shakespeare—and this is not just our question I am suggesting but his—it is worth adding in the context of the play's own struggle for authority that, excluding the history plays, there are two Williams in Shakespeare, both of whom are equally suggestive of their author and both of whom appear just after *Julius Caesar.* In *The Merry Wives of Windsor* (1600?) William Page, son of George Page, enters for a comic

Latin lesson (4.1). His proper names speak for themselves, and Page
and author are brought together in a further reference to William Lily,
author of Lily's *Grammar*. The other William is the rustic William in
As You Like It (1599), who enters just as briefly to woo Audrey.
Undone by Touchstone, he withdraws into the forest of Arden. This
proper name—Arden, Shakespeare's mother's—situates the forest's
difference from the court in terms of Cleopatra's difference from
patriarchy, but with this obvious and important difference: *As You
Like It* is not a tragedy. Duke Frederick invades for his brother in the
final act with all the determination of Caesar but is converted by the
forest, rather than the reverse. The sexual difference revealed by Rosalind's disguise is, moreover, stable, a disguise. Shakespeare's comedies push the figure-power dialectic to its same absolute limits but
only to mock or subvert them. The Pageant of the Nine Worthies in
the closing scene of *Love's Labor's Lost*—Costard's "Pompey the
Big"—is only the most famous example. Rosalind herself draws the
distinction when she likens the suddenness of her cousin Celia's wed-
ding to "Caesar's thrasonical brag of 'I came, saw, and overcame'"
(5.2.31–32; Falstaff's "Caesar, Keiser, and Pheazar," *The Merry Wives
of Windsor*, 1.3.9–10).[12]

When I juxtapose Jakobson on Saussure with Shakespeare on Caesar, I want to underscore the specular or obverse relation joining theory to theater, but I also want to emphasize the way Shakespeare's
function in Jakobson's essay is similar to Caesar's function in *Julius
Caesar*. I want to suggest now that the same relation is in fact true for
a wide range of literary theory, that the figure-power dialectic internalized by Shakespeare's plays is, as such, a feature of their reading as
well, only in reverse. In the play's composition the dialectic accounts
for its particular figuration of power; in its reading the same dialectic
accounts for the (consequently) illimitable power of its figuration.
This is Shakespeare's importance for criticism but also his danger. His
danger—and Marx in his own unlimited enthusiasm for Shakespeare
probably understood this better than anyone—is also his importance.
Both are in evidence when Jakobson remarks how "the trope becomes
a part of poetic reality" in Antony's

> My heart is in the coffin there with Caesar,
> And I must pause till it come back to me.

Antony's *pause* takes the *heart* metonymy literally, but there is
another trope governing the lines, and governing the pause itself. This
is the figure of prosopopeia, the *sta viator*, or "voice-from-beyond-the-

grave," as de Man characterizes the term in "Autobiography as De-Facement" (*Rhetoric of Romanticism*). I mention the trope now because it is along this figure that authority is transferred in Jakobson's essay, from Saussure to Jakobson but also from Shakespeare to structural linguistics. I mention de Man's essay on autobiography because in it, too, Shakespeare functions as a kind of limit, as de Man suggests during a discussion of Milton's memorial lines to Shakespeare:

> Then thou our fancy of itself bereaving,
> Dost make us marble with too much conceiving.

Shakespeare represents a subjective limit for the essay at a particular moment in it, when "Milton speaks of the burden that Shakespeare's 'easy numbers' represent for those who are, like all of us, capable only of 'slow endeavoring art'" (AD, 78). Prosopopeia is the-voice-from-beyond-the-grave, but behind or containing that, de Man implies, and issuing from the subject of autobiography itself, are Shakespeare's "easy numbers." Jakobson's identification with Antony indicates for synchronic poetics how an increase in autobiography converges on an increased presence of the Shakespearean subject, as de Man's essay on autobiography converges on Shakespeare, but the same relation could, again, be developed across a wide range of literary theory. "Is it I," Hélène Cixous writes in the closing pages of her "Sorties" in *The Newly Born Woman*, "when at the thought of Octavia—because she kept you far from our bed, had all the governments and thrones been thrown at my feet, and all Asia added to Egypt to spread my power . . . Is that me? . . . O my husband-mother . . . I no longer recognize myself! But now I know myself."[13] More tentatively, perhaps, Freud's comments in *The Interpretation of Dreams* make clear the extent to which Shakespeare was the authority from whom his own oedipal theory was derived. *Hamlet* instantiates the archetypal Oedipus myth, but Freud's own theory, continuing that tradition, holds the mirror up to *Hamlet*, uncovering the origin of its guilt in a repetition that has all the earmarks of the play's own dumb show ("the image of a murther done in Vienna").[14] Marx in *The Eighteenth Brumaire of Louis Bonaparte* wrestles with the same authority, one who precedes or subsumes class difference in the way Freud's preoedipal subject precedes sexual difference. Hence the book's exuberant vision of the revolution, now submerged and "making its way through purgatory," surfacing one day victorious, when "Europe will leap from its seat and cry in triumph, 'Well burrowed, old mole!'"—but hence, too, its image of the nephew-turned-emperor "behind the iron death mask of Napoleon" while "the old dates rise up again, the old chronology, the old names, the old edicts."[15]

In *Antony and Cleopatra* Shakespeare *stages* the play's own difference from the history, ancient and contemporary, it brings to expression, and the play itself regularly suggests how Egypt's difference from Rome rehearses the play's own difference from the historical and cultural imperatives of its day. Cleopatra's "I shall see / Some squeaking Cleopatra boy my greatness / I' th' posture of a whore" (5.2.219–21) resembles nothing in the play so nearly as her earlier "Shall they hoist me up, / And show me to the shouting varlotry / Of censuring Rome?" (55–57). When the ghost of Hercules departs Antony on the eve of battle, a sentry remarks, "It signs well, does it not?" (5.3.14), and the reference is to the sign of Hercules outside the Globe, "Hercules and his load," as Rosencrantz remarks in a corresponding allusion from *Hamlet* (Cleopatra's "little O, the earth"). In the play's opening scene the lovers jest while Caesar's messenger stands idly by:

> *Antony:*   What sport to-night?
> *Cleopatra:* Hear the ambassadors.
> *Antony:*   Fie, wrangling queen!
>
> (47–48)

The suggestion that "the ambassadors" constitute a kind of theater is largely a joke at Caesar's expense, but it also makes explicit the purely formal relation to an audience that brings together Caesar's messengers and Shakespeare's company, the King's Men. The excessive theatricality of Cleopatra needs to be read, again, against the London stage, and the domestic Rome of Fulvia, and finally Octavia, against Stratford. Such juxtapositions make Shakespeare important for an investigation of theory's relation to power, or figure's relation to structures of domination, but they also complicate any perspective, Shakespeare's included, on the power shaping the relations themselves. In Antony's reference to Caesar's "all-obeying" power it is impossible to determine whether the ambiguity of "all-obeying / obeying all" results from a fondness for wordplay or from a profound engagement with the paradoxes of absolute power. When the elder Caesar is assassinated in *Julius Caesar,* the magnificent shout of Cinna, "Liberty! Freedom! Tyranny is dead!" (3.1.78), could sound to the ears of an audience, and not the eyes of a reader, like "Liberty, Freedom, Tyranny is dead!" The reading that these and other such moments give rise to, that Shakespeare believed the strong rule of a single mastermind was the only hope for civilization, has in fact been regularly offered, but does it spring on Shakespeare's part from a commitment to rhetoric—the delayed-fuse effect of "Liberty . . . is dead" functions in thousands of lines by Shakespeare—or from an engagement with power? The difference is easily overlooked, as the confusion of Cinna the poet and Cinna the conspirator makes clear ("Tear him for his bad verses, tear him for his bad verses" [3.3.30–31]).[16]

What makes the difference so difficult to read, even unreadable, is that the violence it provokes is itself produced as a reading. This at least is de Man's position in later essays but also Shakespeare's position, or Brutus's, at a crucial juncture late in *Julius Caesar:*

> Let me see, let me see; is not the leaf turn'd down
> Where I left reading? Here it is, I think.
> *Enter the Ghost of Caesar.*
>
> (4.3.273–74)

Three things are possible here: Caesar's ghost returns when reading is resumed; his ghost returns when reading is left off; his ghost returns when reading is both resumed and left off. This last position brings the play closest to the theory, at least as de Man represents it. "The leaf" brings Caesar to life, but that is only because it was a failure to read that killed him in the first place ("If thou read this, O Caesar, thou mayest live" [2.2.15]).[17] At the moment of Caesar's death—"Et tu, Brute?—Then fall, Caesar" (3.1.77)—he speaks through the dead language per se, but like the theory itself as de Man represents it in "The Resistance to Theory," and with reference to Keats's "Fall of Hyperion," "what remains impossible to decide is whether this flourishing is a triumph or a fall" (20). For the play also consistently obscures the difference between the history it describes and the one it performs. What starts out as a question ends as an exclamation when Cassius cries: "How many ages hence / Shall this our lofty scene be acted over / In states unborn and accents yet unknown!" (3.1.111–13)—a shift that again sets the performance at odds with the struggle for historical power it brings to expression, in the play but also in any radically performative theory. This is why Marxist critics of de Man are correct to develop in his later work the close relation to established power made explicit in the early writings, but this is also why, we need to consider now, they may be wrong to stop there.

The importance of Adorno for the controversy surrounding de Man is that he seems to condemn de Man's criticism but to validate his art.[18] Obviously, the opposition of criticism to art is not an opposition to be deployed casually in a discussion of either Adorno or de Man, since so much of their work both questions and insists on the difference. In a late interview with Stefano Rosso that ends *The Resistance to Theory*, de Man remarks how his own "progress from purely linguistic analysis to questions which are really already of a political and ideological nature" is "taking me back to Adorno and to attempts that have been made in that direction in Germany, to certain aspects of Heidegger, and I just feel that one has to face therefore the difficulty of certain explicitly political texts" (121). Whereas Adorno regularly undermines the professed detachment of ahistoric criticism, he, like de Man, is much less prepared than many of his Marxist colleagues to collapse the ostensibly apolitical works of the avant-garde into the reigning imperatives, categorical or otherwise, of this totalizing power. If ideology, by definition, hides where it is least expected, it doesn't necessarily appear where it seems most inevitable. What it does by design, it need not do by default. In a very late essay entitled "Commitment" (1962) Adorno juxtaposes directly political art with "Art for Art's Sake" in terms as close to de Man as to those of his Marxist critics:

> Each of the two alternatives negates itself with the other. Committed art, necessarily detached as art from reality, cancels the distance between the two. "Art for Art's Sake" denies by its absolute claims [*Verabsolutierung*] that ineradicable connection with reality which is the polemical *a priori* of the very attempt to make art autonomous from the real. Between these two poles, the tension in which art has lived in every age till now, is dissolved.[19]

The authentically political work of art doesn't trumpet its commitment to activism, nor does it simply hold the mirror up to nations, as one of de Man's early articles would have it (*Het Vlaamsche Land*, 30 March 1942). In an era of radical reification the historical expresses itself as the negative determinant of either extreme. For Adorno one test of a work's authenticity is that it be attacked with equal intensity by both the left and the right, and here the terms are even closer to de Man. According to Adorno,

> cultural conservatives, who demand that a work of art should say something, join forces with their political opponents against atelic, hermetic works of art. Eulogists of "relevance"

are more likely to find Sartre's *Huis clos* profound than to listen patiently to a text whose language jolts signification and by its very distance from "meaning" revolts in advance against positivist subordination of meaning. (CM, 302)

Adorno has no doubts about the strong reliance of authentically political art on the totalizing powers that be, but Picasso's supposed reply to the Nazi officer who had pointed to *Guernica* and asked, "Did you do that?"—"No, you did"—problematizes rather than proves his involvement. It is hardly a confession, but neither is it an alibi. The line is a fine one, but Adorno attempts to draw it in his conclusion:

> Paul Klee too belongs to any debate about committed and autonomous art: for his work, *écriture* par excellence, has roots in literature and would not have been what it is without them—or if it had not consumed them. During the First World War, or shortly after, Klee drew cartoons of Kaiser Wilhelm as an inhuman iron eater. Later, in 1920, these became—the development can be shown quite clearly—the *Angelus Novus,* the machine angel, who, though he no longer bears any emblem of caricature or commitment, flies far beyond both. The machine angel's enigmatic eyes force the onlooker to try to decide whether he is announcing the culmination of disaster or salvation hidden within it. But, as Walter Benjamin, who owned the drawing, said, he is the angel who does not give but takes. (CM, 318)

For de Man, of course, it is hardly a question of "flying far beyond both." Nor could it ever be so for Adorno, whose description doesn't merely emphasize the flight but its grounding in absolutism. The drawing thus represents an image, too, of the relation of de Man's later work to the early writings, but with an important and necessary qualification. If there is an allegory here for de Man's development from Klee's "inhuman iron eater" to M. H. Abrams's "deconstructive angel," it is immediately more complicated in the case of de Man's later work. For by this time the "machine angel" made from the same iron that feeds power has become de Man's "textual machine of its own constitution *and* performance, its own textual allegory" (AR, 278)—and that, early and late, for better or worse, is *its* power.

Klee's drawing, as Adorno represents it, is the perspective of two perspectives, one of criticism and art, one of both of these and their relation to power. Klee's *Angelus Novus* "no longer bears any emblem of caricature or commitment," but "the development can be shown quite clearly." It is this contradiction that brings the drawing closest to de Man's own *écriture,* for the internalization of a certain figure-power dialectic may make the later work look and feel like the early writings written out so far into the margins that the newspaper is no longer readable, but what is harder to decide is whether the newspaper has disappeared from view because absolutely present, as critics like Terry Eagleton and Frank Lentricchia might argue, or finally erased, as critics like Anselm Haverkamp have suggested, for whom de Man's later work is politically enabling, even revolutionary. Andrzej Warminski has commented how de Man's picture in a *New York Times* article on the wartime writings seemed to a student of his as potentially sinister as the same photograph on the cover of *The Lesson of Paul de Man* looked benign. It is, again, a difficult difference: de Man's later work is still probably far more reactionary than we know, and far more radical. The wartime writings, by deepening the perspective, further blur the distinction. They make explicit the collusion of figure with power submerged or resisted in the later writing, but they also make explicit the resistance.

Nuclear Criticism (the *Aufhebung* of the Sun)

I read Shakespeare directly I have finished writing. When my mind is agape and red-hot. Then it is astonishing. I never yet knew how amazing his stretch and speed and word coining power is, until I felt it utterly outpace and outrace my own, seeming to start equal and then I see him draw ahead and do things I could not in my wildest tumult and utmost press of mind imagine. Even the less known plays are written at a speed that is quicker than any-body else's quickest; and the words drop so fast one can't pick them up. Look at this: "Upon a gather'd lily almost wither'd" (that is a pure accident: I happen to light on it). . . . Why then should anyone else attempt to write? This is not "writing" at all. Indeed, I could say that Shakespeare surpasses literature alto-gether, if I knew what I meant.
                    —*Virginia Woolf,* Diary, *Sunday, 13 April 1930*

That of all literature Shakespeare's "belongs to the nuclear age" receives literal point when René Girard connects the language of deferral in *Hamlet* to the logic of deterrence. "Like Hamlet," Girard suggests of the nuclear situation, "we are poised on the fence between total revenge and no revenge at all, unable to make up our mind, unable to take revenge and yet unable to renounce it."[1] In the course of deciding to drop the bomb on Hiroshima, Truman reread and marked a passage from just this drama of indecisiveness: "But let this scene be presently performed, / Even while men's minds are wild; lest more mischance, / Or plots and errors, happen."[2] As Ken Ruthven observes, "To bomb or not to bomb, that was the question uppermost in Truman's mind."[3] Much more generally, what Derrida says about the atomic properties of Joyce's post-Enlightenment language in "Two Words for Joyce" proves even more true, Joyce himself would say, of Shakespeare: "he repeats and mobilizes and babelizes the (asymptotic) totality of the equivocal, he makes this his theme and his operation, he tries to make outcrop, with the greatest possible synchrony, at great speed, the greatest power of the meanings buried in each syllabic fragment, subjecting each atom of writing to fission in order to overload the unconscious with the whole memory of man: mythologies, religion, philosophies, sciences, psychoanalysis, literatures."⁴ In Derrida's essay "Aphorism Countertime," a fundamental iterability in *Romeo and Juliet* lends the play a temporality every bit as relative and fragmentary as the one described by nuclear physics:

> What Romeo and Juliet experience is the exemplary anachrony, the essential impossibility of any absolute synchronization. But *at the same time* they live—as we do—this disorder of the series. Disjunction, dislocation, separation of places, deployment or spacing of a story because of aphorism—would there be any theater without that? The survival of the theatrical work implies that, theatrically, it is saying something about the theater itself, about its essential possibility.⁵

Shakespeare's penchant for punning, the fatal Cleopatra, the nucleopatra, the nuc-Lear, for which he gave the world, threatens ours.

In Shakespeare, too, the unprecedented speed of the language converges on an equally idealized, and idealizing, light. In early plays the lines of association are closely generic, historic, or lyrical. The notorious sun-king associations of *Richard II* give way to Romeo's "It is the east, and Juliet is the sun" (2.2.3) in a counter lyric of the same year (1596). A third play from 1594–95, *A Midsummer Night's Dream*, reaffirms lyrically the troubled *roi-soleil* associations of *Richard II* (Titania's "The summer still doth tend upon my state" [3.1.155]) while distancing the symmetrical violence of star-crossed lovers by emphasizing the figural incongruousness of the "man i' th' moon" cast over the rude mechanicals' "Pyramus and Thisby" ("Tongue, lose thy light, / Moon, take thy flight" [5.1.304–5]). In *The Taming of the Shrew*, also from 1594, the distracted heavens of Kate's capitulation to Petruchio—"Then God be blest, it is the blessed sun, / But sun it is not, when you say it is not; / And the moon changes even as your mind" (4.5.18–20)—are already restored by her moonlike capitulation before the "sun" of patriarchy, as Petruchio, again, homonymically insists: "Now by my mother's son, and that's myself, / It shall be moon, or star, or what I list" (6–7). This cosmic order-in-disorder also characterizes the play's subplot, as Fineman observes in his essay "The Turn of the Shrew":

The mixup of fathers is definitively resolved when Lucentio, until then disguised as Cambio, kneels down before his father and reveals his proper self. "Cambio is changed into Lucentio" (5.1.123) is the line with which this final revelation is theatrically announced, and it can serve as an economical example of the way in which, in Shakespearean comedy, it is possible for the principle of linguistic "change" itself to change into "light" on condition that "change" itself is treated as something merely witty or absurd. Translation, transformation, disguise, metamorphosis, all such instances and operations of difference serve, when developed in this comic way, to reestablish the serious hierarchy governed by a patriarchal sun.[6]

Later plays are later (and generally darker) as the subject's relation to light is less ideal—too far or too near, as in Macbeth's "Scarf up the tender eye of pitiful day" (3.2.47) or Cleopatra's "O sun, / Burn the great sphere thou mov'st in" (4.15.9–10)—this last apostrophe to an exploding helios from a play whose mythological tableau of Roman sun and Egyptian moon re-distances lyrically the more sharply psychological eclipses ushered in by *Hamlet* ("The night is joint-laborer with the day" [1.1.78]), *Othello* ("Hell and night / Must bring this monstrous birth to the world's light" [1.3.403–4]), *King Lear* ("These late eclipses in the sun and moon" [1.2.103]), and *Macbeth* ("By the clock 'tis day, / And yet dark night strangles the travelling lamp"). If, at the traditional midpoint of Shakespeare's dramatic trajectory, Hamlet represents the virtual epiphany of the Shakespearean subject, the observed of all observers, his inky cloak and stagy darkness remain as it were the *condition* of his being "too much in the sun" (1.2.67).

Tropically, too, the temporality underwriting the nuclear equation underwrites the poetry. In Aristotle's archetypal metaphor by analogy, "night is the old age of day," one temporal duration (a day) momentarily glosses over another (a lifetime) even as light itself, the temporal limit in physics from which unfold an infinite number of discrete temporal frames or durations at every velocity relative to light, glosses over life. But even in a metaphor whose terms are not temporally allied, as in Aristotle's companion example of *the cup of Mars* for *shield* or *the shield of Bacchus* for *cup*, the two relations result from iterative (and therefore time-bound) associations of the shield with Mars and the cup with Bacchus, just as both associations are themselves metonymic. This temporality, in turn, characterizes not just metaphor and metonymy in Shakespeare but, with almost equal significance, paradox and irony: whereas paradox entails the ostensible coexistence of discrete temporal references ("My only love sprung from my only hate!" [*Romeo and Juliet*, 1.5.138]), irony introduces a momentary difference into temporal simultaneity ("But I should kill thee with much cherishing" [2.2.184]). Shakespeare's sonnets, too, literally declare war on time, but their very permanence, paradoxically, ironically, and metonymically, derives from their own irreducible temporality ("Now with the drops of this most balmy time"). In "Give my love fame faster than time wastes life" (100) the various internal resonances—*give/love, love/life, life/fame, fame/time, time/my, my/life, life/fast, fast/wastes, wastes/give*—add more time to the reading than a reading can ever contain in a literal (because *absolutely* figural) race against time, a speed limit (100) that all subsequent writing, Woolf's or Joyce's, henceforth approximates. As Howard Felperin remarks of the sonnets' paradoxical transcendence of temporality in and through time, "by reactivating through wordplay . . . decayed senses and pressing them into the service of his writing, Shakespeare imagines himself defeating Time and Death at their own war-game. . . . What Shakespeare has done is to include the work of time within his own work in such a way as to arrest flux and pre-empt obsolescence."[7] From the otherwise incongruous discussions of father time's "bald lock" in *The Comedy of Errors* (2.2.70–108) to the literalizing *Tempest*, time represents the limit subject, being *as* time, embodied by the gap-bridging Chorus/Kronos of Shakespeare's penultimate (and again temporally designated) *Winter's Tale*. For if time exists, or to the extent that it exists, it has always existed, since there can never be anything *before* time (time being a necessary condition of just this "before" time). And as time has always existed it will also always exist, since there can never be anything *after* time (time being a necessary condition of just this "after" time). Time is, then, but only because it has always been and will always be, now here because nowhere. In the process, the distortion of time as velocity approaches light, and its disappearance at the limit velocity light, necessarily opens up an infinite field or continuum of discrete temporal horizons (discrete "moments," themselves infinite in number) as velocity increases with respect to light. Thus, if there is light there is temporality, and if there is temporality there is figure, and if there is figure there is thought—the first thought, "*fiat lux*," let there be time.

In his essay "No Apocalypse, Not Now (full speed ahead: seven missiles, seven missives)" Derrida notes how the question of nuclear war is in fact inseparable from the question of "literature." In the first place "a total nuclear war," as Derrida considers it, "has no precedent.

It has never occurred, itself; it is a non-event," a speculum or fable, "a fantasy, a phantasm" (24). Even the event itself would only extend the performative horizon it paradoxically shatters, since the very passage into reference corresponds, in this case, to a blasting away of the archive, of the whole symbolic field. The nuclear age thus shares the irreducibly figural or rhetorical horizon marked out by deconstruction ("deconstruction . . . belongs to the nuclear age").[8]

Literature, too, "by virtue of the performative character of its relation to the referent," has always belonged to the nuclear age. To cite only one particular example from what may be the great American novel (this, at least, may have been Melville's judgment, author of the putative favorite *Moby-Dick*), at about the exact middle of Hawthorne's *House of the Seven Gables* Clifford and Phoebe Pyncheon are looking out from "the arched window," which is also the name of the chapter. "One afternoon," Hawthorne writes, "a scissor-grinder chanced to set his wheel agoing under the Pyncheon Elm, and just in front of the arched window. . . . Round went the busily revolving machinery, kept in motion by the scissor-grinder's foot."[9] Here, at the center of Hawthorne's narrative, whirls the mechanized wheel that so fixes Rousseau and marks, for de Man, the intrusion or the insertion of chance (Hawthorne's "chanced"); four years later Hawthorne's "busily revolving machinery" becomes the gigantic text-as-killing-machine of Melville's paper mill in "The Paradise of Bachelors and the Tartarus of Maids": "Round and round here went the enormous revolutions of the dark colossal waterwheel, grim with its one immutable purpose."[10] Outside the arched window on other days, Hawthorne writes, sometimes "one of those Italian boys (who are rather a modern feature of our streets) came along with his barrel organ, and stopped under the wide and cool shadows of the elm." Summing up the organist's "splendid attractions," "there was a company of little figures, whose sphere and habitation was in the mahogany case of his organ, and whose principle of life was the music which the Italian made it his business to grind out." The same verb, *grind*, mechanically links the first scene with the second, but now the machine figures more directly, like a shield, the story that contains it. When, near the close of the novel, the organist again appears before the Pyncheon house, now empty except for the dead Jaffrey Pyncheon, the "hurdy-gurdy" figures, too, a technology that kills, taking in, again, all the principals of the narrative: "The Italian turned a crank, and behold! . . . The cobbler wrought upon a shoe; the blacksmith hammered his iron; . . . a scholar . . . turned his head to and fro along the page" (145).

Hawthorne's whirling wheel turned killing machine typifies literature's special affinity with a properly nuclear technology, but the same technology, Derrida's seven missiles affirm, characterizes the theory as well. Indeed, the history of ideas may one day come to read deconstruction as the mock-apocalyptic, hyper-ironic inversion of a bygone nuclear age, and so contain it, in order to take up again the history of ideas. Thus, when Derrida remarks how "one may still die after having spent one's life recognizing, as a lucid historian, to what extent all that was not new, telling oneself that the inventors of the nuclear age or of nuclear criticism did not invent the wheel, or, as we say in French, 'invent gunpowder'" (21), the issue of nationalism called up by "as we say in French" is a reminder that this same race for speed drives interpretation, whether represented by the lucid historian or by nuclear criticism, a criticism always, today, in danger of rushing to the exact same unavoidable conclusion. "It's what we call in French a *course de vitesse,* a *speed race*" (20), Derrida writes, and the French, the *course de vitesse,* always comes before the *speed race* (just as, in Derrida's original text, the English *speed race* always comes after the French *course de vitesse).*

Deconstruction is thus properly "French" to the extent that, in the United States, the unspeakable potential of the nuclear situation has almost displaced, as the locus of a mass psychic resistance, of an astronomical state secret, the unspeakable past of the Indian genocide, a shift that prefigures something like the Tomahawk cruise missile but that the so-called red scare which ushered in the arms race had already set in motion, leaving the erstwhile "redskins" to take up residence in the nation's capital disguised as a football team—to "intercept the bomb," up on the screen, there. For underneath the nationalism is the acceleration, which is like the land to the ideology, not the presidents but the mountain, Mount Rush-more. Nowhere is there participation or control: consensus is gone and replaced by technology, and the technology is classified. Even the tests are underground. This unconscious, this properly nuclear unconscious, the industrial-military complex, Freud might have called it, locked as it is on that point where the dreamwork plunges into the unknown (as the saying goes) like a mushroom growing out of its mycelium, this unconscious, today, "touches every atom of our being" (20). Deterrence, too, is consensus by default. The bomb's very power makes it disempowering, the phallic icon, as a number of commentaries dutifully attest, of an absolute leveling or castration. That nuclear strategy dovetails with aberrant sexual desire is not just a theme of *Dr. Strangelove* but also the point of the name, Strange-love (the "bikini," then, named for the Pacific atoll destroyed by a nuclear test in 1947 by way of [Webster] "the atomic effect produced by the first bikini"). The phallic preponderance of Pynchon's *Gravity's Rainbow* marks a similar conjunction in a novel that brings Hawthorne's preliminary technology, his "organ," into the nuclear age; indeed, Pynchon is a direct descendant of the Thomas Ruggles Pyncheon who, in a letter to Hawthorne following publication of *The House of the Seven Gables*, complained of abuses to the family name ("It occurs to Slothrop here that without those horns on it, why his helmet would look just like . . . the Rocket. And if he could find a few triangular scraps of leather . . . yeah, and on the back of the cape put a big, scarlet, capital R").[11] This phallicness, in turn, further underwrites the bomb's Cold War fetishization by the military—the blinding basilisk or Medusa, the bombshell—in a uniquely male *hysteria*.

Derrida delivered his comments at a conference on "nuclear criticism" conducted at Cornell University in 1984. This symposium, this nuclear exchange, culminates in Derrida's seven missiles, or missives, and the seven interrelated questions they raise. Each section of the essay, seven in all, begins or ends with an italicized aphorism or statement of position, such as *"In the beginning there will have been speed"* (20) or, more essentially, *"The name of nuclear war is the name of the first war which can be fought in the name of the name alone, that is, of everything and of nothing"* (30). These are the detonations. So *denotated*, deconstruction already represents a kind of physics, as Gregory Ulmer and Floyd Merrell have noted, effecting the expulsion, or the explosion, of the "meta" and all it represents—transcendence, priority, opposition, depth—from metaphysics.[12] "Beyond the philosophical text," Derrida writes in the preface to *Margins*, "there is not a blank, virgin, empty margin, but another text, a weave of differences of forces without any present center of reference."[13] Derrida thus speaks favorably to "the discord of the different forces and of the differences between forces which Nietzsche opposes to the entire system of metaphysical grammar, wherever that system controls culture, philosophy, and science" (149). This second text, then, speaks through the silences of the first, even to the mute *s* of Derrida's essay on *anasemia*, "Fors."[14] The tremendous leveling power of the nuclear equation corresponds, in turn, to the closest possible translation of this second text by the first, of force by signification, even as the race of force and signification that constitutes deconstructive writing reaches its most intense literalization (its maximum speed) in the equations of nuclear physics. This is why *différance* so effortlessly recuperates for metaphysics the function of the limit velocity, light, in physics—at once spatial and temporal ("the latter [*différance*] (is) (both) spacing (and) temporalizing"); matter and energy ("life as differing-differed matter; mind as differed-differing life"); particle and wave ("no longer simply a concept but the possibility of conceptuality"). For Derrida, too, "the Einsteinian constant is not a constant, is not a center. It is the very concept of variability—it is, finally, the concept of the game."[15] As Ulmer observes:

> Derrida is redefining the idea, working on its root metaphor of sight and light, analyzing it no longer in terms of its effect (the light bulb that lights up when we have an idea in cartoons and advertisements) but in terms of its physics, energy waves (the vibrations mediated by air, the level at which light and sound are equivalents, identified in relation to the body in terms of the "objective senses" of sight and hearing).[16]

In similar terms the elective affinity of physics within and across the entire spectrum of poststructuralist writing could thereby be developed, from Freud's early preoccupation with Fechner's experiments in electromagnetism to Adorno's ever-present "force field" to Michel Serres's "thermodynamics," his "history of the sun" (*Hermes* I–III).

Like the subliminal in physics, the sublime in metaphysics, what Frances Ferguson has called "the nuclear sublime," thus names the excession of all representation by force.[17] In an essay on the sublime in Hegel, de Man notes how Hegel's earliest illustration of figure, the *fiat lux* of *Genesis*, is held to a second example, four pages later in the *Aesthetics*, by a parallel phrasing de Man finds (since it is a question of the sublime) "amazing."[18] The first quotation, *fiat lux*, issues from God, or as Hegel writes, "von Seiten Gottes her"; the second, "Light is your garment, that you wear; you stretch out the heavens like a curtain," issues from man, or as Hegel writes four pages later, "von Seiten des Menschen."

De Man's essay closely follows Neil Hertz's "A Reading of Longinus," an essay de Man pronounces (since, again, it is a question of the sublime) "remarkable." Hertz, too, begins with the *fiat lux* of Longinus; his second illustration of the sublime is the very next illustration in Longinus, "from the human sphere this time":

> Darkness falls suddenly. Thickest night blinds the Greek army. Ajax is bewildered. "O father Zeus," he cries,

"Deliver the sons of the Achaeans out of the mist,
Make the sky clear, and let us see;
In the light—kill us."[19]

Hertz follows this quotation with sentences that explicitly displace those following in Longinus:

> The sentences that follow comment on the truthfulness of these lines as a representation of Ajax' feeling, yet they make nothing of what is most striking about the juxtaposition of these two fragments: that they are both calls for light—one on the part of a god, associated with the creative act; the other, on the part of a mortal, at the risk of his own destruction.

Hegel's "von Seiten Gottes her" / "von Seiten des Menschen" here returns to Hertz's "on the part of a god" / "on the part of a mortal," but in his discussion of Hegel's parallel phrasing de Man nowhere mentions the same parallel phrasing in Hertz's echo of Hegel's echo, which, across volumes and even centuries, is perhaps more amazing than Hegel's parallel phrasing across four pages of the *Aesthetics;* at the very least, it is "striking," as Hertz finds the silent juxtaposition of light in Longinus. Light, then, functions as a limit not just in but for each of the four readings (de Man's "the divergence between Hegel and Longinus becomes nearly as absolute as the divergence between man and God Hegel calls sublime" [149]).

Fiat lux, then, "the one instance of sublimity that Hegel and Longinus share in common," as de Man notes, and therefore the one instance of sublimity common to all four readings, is not merely sublime; the first imperative, it also literalizes the sublime, "parting" force and signification. Viewed in *this* light, the de Manian deconstruction that perpetually puts the force-signification opposition into play is the other side of a nuclear knowledge that can never be entirely repressed or eliminated, as Derrida suggests in his essay on de Man's own wartime journalism, "Biodegradables: Seven Diary Fragments": "It's as if something nonbiodegradable had been submerged at the bottom of the sea. It irradiates. . . ."[20] For Derrida "the entire history of our philosophy is a photology, the name given to a history of, or treatise on, light," and again, "each time that there is a metaphor, there is doubtless a sun somewhere" (*Margins,* 251), but the nuclear pharmakon brings this photology to the surface, literalizing the sublime (the sublimation of force by signification).[21]

From the side of physics, on the other hand, this same parallel phrasing of light can be seen by developing the strictly formal impli-cations of a representative equation. The following, for example, is Einstein's equation for relative mass, where m_r = relative mass, m_o = ordinary (rest) mass, v = velocity, and c = the speed of light:

$$m_r = \frac{m_o}{\sqrt{1 - \dfrac{v^2}{c^2}}}$$

When velocity is zero (the world of Newtonian physics), relative mass and ordinary mass are the same, since the denominator on the right side of the equation equals one. As velocity increases, relative mass grows larger with respect to rest mass. At $v = c$ the denominator goes to zero and m_r is infinite. This is a staple of relativity: nothing can travel at the speed of light because to do that its mass would have to be infinite. Beyond that limit, when velocity exceeds the speed of light, the denominator on the right side of the equation becomes the square root of a negative number, becomes an imaginary number. At $v > c$ the value for relative mass is an imaginary number. As it is in the case of the sublime, the speed of light is thus a barrier, the upper limit for velocities in a physical universe, the lower limit for matter whose hypothetical mass is an imaginary number:

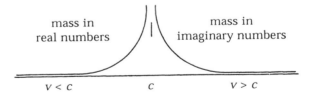

Insofar as parallel curves approaching but never appropriating light describe the aporia of the Hegelian sublime, which also takes the form of a parallel phrasing, light, as "the Aufhebung of natural exteri-ority," as an *Aufhebung* of the sign ("the process of the sign is an Aufhebung" [*Margins*, 88]), has already taken the form of the double apostrophe that characterizes its appearance in the literature of the sublime. Obviously, the place of the middle mark designated by c is of some importance, that mathematical limit where a real object is translated, at the speed of light, into its imaginary counterpart. We may reserve a certain *scientistic* taxonomy and call it here, provisionally, the retina.

Within the postwar university, then, the nuclear equation levels as well the language of metaphysics and the language of physics—the nuclear terrorist, finally, as poststructural Unabomber. Shakespeare thus delimits nuclear criticism, which in turn delimits postwar criticism and theory, because in Shakespeare the logos of the dream and of the *theos* and of literature is not the father but the light, not the slaying at the crossroads but, still by Apollo, the blinding (Claudius's "Lights, lights, lights!" [3.2.270]). In *Hamlet* above all, as Girard observes, literature speaks to the irreducible otherness of the nuclear referent, and to a criticism on the brink, to the critical necessity of both slowing down and accelerating the proliferation of figures—"turns of phrases, tropes and strophes"—that, in their turn, precipitate and circumvent "the inevitable catastrophe." So, at the self-described dawn-turned-dusk of the information age, it remains for a nuclear criticism to make clear how the nuclear equation represents the corresponding limit or fold that governs everywhere today, everywhere *and* more and more, all this writing with light, this photography—up on the screen, there.

At the limit velocity, light, time ceases. This, too, is a staple of relativity. So is the familiar twin paradox that regularly serves to illustrate the slowing of time as velocity increases relative to light. Thus, Mike and Ike or Pho and Thon, traveling in separate rockets at widely different velocities, age at different rates, even until the younger twin, again after *Hamlet*, is the older. This rocket science race for the birthright would be little more than a sendup of Jacob and Esau, biblical parody, if, today, its hackneyed reworking of Revelations weren't itself something of an extraordinary literalization, biblical *parity*. More and more, the negative dialectic is uncovering in the origin of life its limits. Every decade or so a new nation joins the nuclear family. For, while the ultimate risk of an all-out nuclear encounter is certainly lower today than it was before the end of the Cold War and the fall of the Soviet empire, it is also probably higher. This is why the inclusion of physics among the human sciences can never represent one methodological shift among others, even as its seriousness will always be tested, and tested in light of the nuclear situation, which makes light of everything. At the nuclear limit history goes to zero the way that time goes to zero at the limit velocity light, a limit that not only oversees the nuclear calculus, the after-math, but surfaces, in its greatest possible human expression, in the event. This is what makes the question of nuclear criticism at once so pressing and so temporary, since the cataclysm itself, at the detemporalized limit, has already started. And it is over. No prophecy is more natural, or more extreme, than the end of the world, for that is where prophecy begins, with the overcoming of history, with the end of the world. At the end of the world there will have been prophecy.

At the beginning there will have been speed.

Cultural Studies: Shakespeare and the Beatles

At first glance Shakespeare and the Beatles would seem to have a few things in common, principally the sheer popularity of their lyrics. The Beatles were, in John Lennon's words, "the greatest show on earth," and in this they harnessed the tremendous cultural and historical energies that made of Shakespeare's own poetry and plays a kind of living theater. Much more immediately, however, the Beatles' album *Sgt. Pepper's Lonely Hearts Club Band* (1967) casts Shakespeare himself in the role of lead singer, or fifth Beatle, as the opening title song ends and the album's second song, "With a Little Help from My Friends," begins:

> I don't really want to stop the show
> But I thought you might like to know
> That the singer's gonna sing a song
> And he wants you all to sing along
> So let me introduce to you
> The one and only Billy Shears
> And Sgt. Pepper's Lonely Hearts Club Band
> BILLY SHEARS![1]

Here, to the cheers of a background audience, Ringo Starr steps forth to sing "With a Little Help from My Friends":

> What would you think if I sang out of tune
> Would you stand up and walk out on me
> Lend me your ears and I'll sing you a song
> And I'll try not to sing out of key.

In a 1974 interview with *Rolling Stone* magazine Paul McCartney suggested that the name Billy Shears had no particular significance but was selected merely for the sake of sound.[2] Nevertheless, "Billy Shears" makes William Shakespeare the lead singer on what is normally considered the most important or representative album in rock-and-roll history, such as it is but perhaps such as it always will be; the fictional singer's initial appeal to the audience, "Lend me your ears and I'll sing you a song," further recalls *Julius Caesar,* as if Shakespeare and the Beatles were competing for the same popular audience—"Lend me your ears and *I'll* sing you a song." Thus, while Shakespeare is conspicuously absent from the gallery of notables on the album's famous cover, he is in effect the only one of them to make an appearance on the record itself, and even more grandly than the opening Abraham Lincoln of "Four score and seven years ago" turned "It was twenty years ago today / Sgt. Pepper taught the band to play," itself a distant recollection of King Lear's "Fourscore and upward, not an hour more nor less" (4.7.60)—hence, in the Beatles' animated military film of 1968, *Yellow Submarine,* "Four scores and seven bars ago."

The album *Sgt. Pepper* thus introduces Shakespeare himself, Billy Shears, to its imaginary audience ("So let me introduce to you"), but it also introduces, I want to suggest, a quasi-Shakespearean fusion of first and second person, *me* and *you.* In Shakespeare's sonnets the repeated association of the poet's desire ("my love") with the object of that desire ("my love") most abbreviates this seamless identification of first and second person, *my love* and *my love:*

> When that mine eye is famished for a look,
> Or heart in love with sighs himself doth smother,
> With *my love's* picture then my eye doth feast,
> And to the painted banquet bids my heart.
> Another time mine eye is my heart's guest,
> And in his thoughts of love doth share a part.
> So either by thy picture or *my love,*
> Thyself away are present still with me.
>
> (47.3–10)

Making the picture the poem, *ut pictura poesis,* the transformation of *my love* into *my love* extends to the poem's second second person, the reader: "So either by thy picture [the poem] or my love." In sonnet 105 *my love* (desire) further balances *my love* (the beloved) even as *my songs* balance *my verse,* as if the poem's loss of "difference" somehow included the difference between *my love* and *my songs:*

Let not *my love* be called idolatry,
Nor my beloved as an idol show,
Since all alike *my songs* and praises be,
To one, of one, still such, and ever so.
Kind is *my love* today, tomorrow kind,
Still constant in a wondrous excellence;
Therefore *my verse*, to constancy confined,
One thing expressing, leaves out difference.

(1–8)

Like *my love* and *my love*, *To one, of one* inscribes or literalizes the same paradoxical two-in-oneness as *wondrous excellence*, whose *one* is once again two (*wondrous*) after the fashion of Lennon's "I'm a Loser" (1964): "Of all the love I have *won* and have lost / There is *one* love I should never have crossed"—hence, for example, "*When* the battle's lost and *won*" (*Macbeth*, 1.1.4).

In the case of "my love" and the Beatles, McCartney's "And I Love Her" (1964) is perhaps the most straightforward of early examples:

I give her all *my love*
That's all I do
And if you saw *my love*
You'd love her too
I love her.

Here the shift from *my love* as desire to *my love* as the object of desire parallels a second shift from *her* ("I give *her* all my love") to *you* ("And if *you* saw my love"), a substitution of the listener for the beloved that the song's bridge somewhat remarkably makes explicit:

A love like ours
Could never die
As long as I
Have you near me.

The song's title, "And I Love Her," would seem to preclude the fourth line's substitution of *you* for *her*. The wit is all "ours," since *ours* allows both *her* and *you* to be addressed long enough to effect the substitution of one for the other. As the song progresses, the *you* addressed in the opening stanzas (the listener) becomes the object of affection (the beloved). The process beginning to unfold here is thus a very dear one to the Beatles, for what the lyric brings to the surface is the unspoken identification of the listener and the beloved at work, I want to suggest, in every Beatle lyric, from "Listen / Do you want to know a secret" (1964) to "Listen to the music playing in your head" ("Lady Madonna" [1969]). For even in the earliest Beatle songs this movement from first person to second, "From Me to You" (the title of a Beatle song from 1963), becomes a confusions of *yous* and *mes* but one very different from the "all together now" imperative of later lyrics like Lennon's "I Am the Walrus" ("I am he as you are he as you are me and we are all together"). The third songs on either side of the album *Rubber Soul* (1965), "I'm Looking through You" and "You Won't See Me," hold up the two extremes that actually meet in such a relation:

"I'M LOOKING THROUGH YOU"

I'm looking through you
Where did you go
I thought I knew you
What did I know
You don't look different but you have changed
I'm looking through you
You're not the same.

"YOU WON'T SEE ME"

When I call you up
Your line's engaged
I have had enough
So act your age
We have lost the time that was so hard to find
And I will lose my mind
If you won't see me.

In both lyrics the *you* is the usual young lady but one who cannot be reached, or, in what amounts to the same thing, is already "engaged." Most of the songs on *Rubber Soul* are written around their own potential isolation with respect to these shifting poles of sender and receiver, as in "Girl" ("Is there anybody going to listen to my story"), or "Michelle" ("I will say the only words I know that you'll understand"), whose *you,* again, can never be the *you* of the lyric, who understands only French. The album ends on a similar note with Lennon's "Run for Your Life," which begins:

> Well I'd rather see you dead little girl
> Than to be with another man
> You better keep your head little girl
> Or I won't know where I am
> You better run for your life if you can little girl,

and which ends:

> I'd rather see you dead little girl
> Than to be with another man
> You better keep your head little girl
> Or you won't know where I am
> You better run for your life if you can little girl.

The shift from *I* to *you* in the fourth line is partly a modest kind of wordplay: "I won't know where I am" describes the being-beside-one-self of jealousy and "you won't know where I am" the response. But it is also the other or darker side of the same displacement of *you* that produces desire, the "nowhere" in "know where" ("I'm looking through you / And I don't know where") that names the vanishing point of these self-canceling relations not explicitly foregrounded until "Nowhere Man" (1965)—"Isn't he a bit like you and me" ("Knows not where he's going"). In a related song from 1967, George Harrison's "Only a Northern Song," this disappearing subject is still more immediately the self of the lyric:

> If you think the harmony
> Is a little dark and out of key
> You're correct
> There's nobody there
> And I told you there's no one there.

Harrison's "There's nobody there" also echoes a song from 1966, McCartney's "Eleanor Rigby," and "Father McKenzie / Darning his socks in the night when there's nobody there." Harrison's next line, "And I told you there's no one there," further recalls Father McKenzie, or McCartney, "Writing the words of a sermon that no one will hear," as if "no one" were the intended listener ("For No One" is the title of another McCartney song from the same album). In a song like "Run for Your Life," on the other hand, what *you* and *I* have in common is that neither one knows for sure "where I am," the deathlike condition or dangerous flip-side of desire that, in what is traditionally called the later Beatles (and the later Shakespeare), subsumes all parties even as the love did—the I, the you, the girl, even the song. "Let me take you down 'cause I'm going to Strawberry Fields / Nothing is real," Lennon remarks in "Strawberry Fields Forever," the virtual theme song of the album *Magical Mystery Tour* (1967), but that's only because "The Magical Mystery Tour / Is dying to take you away / Dying to take you away / Take you today."

From *my love* to *my love*, and from William Shakespeare to Billy Shears, *I* and *you* denote the singer and the beloved but also, inside out, the listener and the song, *you* and *I*. Indeed, in a later song like "Your Mother Should Know" (1967) this simultaneous appeal to a second person inside and outside the lyric would seem to be the point of the entire song:

> Let's all get up and dance to a song
> That was a hit before your mother was born
> Though she was born a long long time ago
> Your mother should know
> Sing it again [*repeat*]
>
> Lift up your hearts and sing me a song
> That was a hit before your mother was born
> Though she was born a long long time ago
> Your mother should know
> Sing it again

Here "Sing it again" refers the listener quite conventionally to the final repeating verse of "Your Mother Should Know," but it also repeats the general injunction of the song, "Lift up your hearts and sing me a song / That was a hit before your mother was born." In "Sing it again" the song your mother should know is no longer separable from the song "Your Mother Should Know." For as soon as this happens, as soon as the old song is the new song and the lyric evolves, by slow degrees, into itself, the *you* addressed throughout is the listener. The mother-to-child relation of song, the *mom* in *pop*, further confounds the listener and beloved (the *baby*, finally, in *baby*) in later lyrics like Lennon's "Julia" (1968), written to his mother ("Half of what I say is meaningless / But I say it just to reach you Julia"), or the more typically universalizing "Mother Mary [McCartney]" of "I wake up to the sound of music / Mother Mary comes to me" in "Let it Be" (1970).

In "Lend me your ears and I'll sing you a song," the relation of first to second person in Shakespeare and the Beatles thus extends to Shakespeare (*Julius Caesar*) and the Beatles (*Sgt. Pepper*). Against a similar Shakespearean backdrop, *Magical Mystery Tour* psychedelically recasts, from the fool on the heath to "The Fool on the Hill," *King Lear* ("The Fool" was also the name of a clothing boutique opened by the Beatles in 1967); in "Penny Lane" the performative logic of "Though she feels as if she's in a play / She is anyway" similarly carries common sense ("the fireman rushes in") and sense ("rushes in from the pouring rain") into Lear-like nonsense ("the fireman rushes in from the pouring rain"). Beyond McCartney's "O that this too too solid flesh would melt" (1.2.129) in the film *Hard Day's Night* (1964), *Hamlet* is more the model for the Who's Beatlesque rock opera *Tommy* (1969), whose Claudius-like murder of a ghostly father makes Tommy go deaf, dumb, and blind as Hamlet goes mad ("I'm your wicked uncle Ernie"); the largest selling album of all time, *Westside Story,* further recasts *Romeo and Juliet.* To similar popular effect, Disney's most successful animated feature, *The Lion King,* retells *Hamlet,* just as the Ariel and Sebastian Crab of Disney's *Little Mermaid* refashion *The Tempest,* and the Iago of Disney's *Aladdin* reworks *Othello.* Hollywood's putative masterpiece, Orson Welles's *Citizen Kane,* modernizes *King Lear* in much the way that Welles's *Chimes at Midnight* autobiographically pastiches the Falstaff plays, while the most popular dramatic series in television history, "Dallas," reworks *Richard III,* with J. R. Ewing—again, J. R. (*you are*) Youing—in the role of Richard. Set in the city of Kennedy's assassination, "Dallas" also harkens back to that violence in much the way that "Beatlemania" has sometimes been ascribed to a culture-wide catharsis in the wake of Kennedy's shooting. Like Lennon, J. R.'s first name is also John; his son, J. R. Jr., is John Ross. His brother's name is Bobby. The television question of the 1980s, then, "Who shot J. R.?" is the television question of a generation: "Who shot John Kennedy?" From J. R. to JFK, in turn, Lennon's own shooting in New York a year later reworks the same Shakespearean violence, and almost literally so in the proleptic lines from a BBC *King Lear* added by Lennon to the closing chorus of "I Am the Walrus" ("Come and get your tan from standing in the English rain")—Oswald's (Lee Harvey Oswald's) "Villain, bury my body. . . . O, untimely death!" (4.6.250), followed by Gloucester's "What, is he dead?" and, as the first side of *Magical Mystery Tour* draws to a close, Edgar's "Sit you down, father; rest you."

So far we have noted how the relation of first person to second in Shakespeare and the Beatles invariably implicates the listener or reader, from the ubiquitous "I love that love song" of postwar popular music to Shakespeare's "Give my love fame faster than time wastes life" (100.13), in which *my love* once again names both the poem and the beloved, as in McCartney's solo "My Love" (1973). Thus, in a song like "Hello Good-bye" (1967), *high, low, hi, hello, why,* and *I don't know* make *you* and *I* ("You say yes / I say no") no more distinct than the vowel sounds *u* and *i* underwriting entire early lyrics like "It's Only Love" (1965)—"*I* get *high* when *I* see *you* go *by* / *Why* am *I* so *shy* when *I'm* be*side you.*" *You* and *I,* in turn, delimit popular culture—and therefore cultural studies—by personifying, even embodying, ongoing historical process; in "Lend me your ears," the one first and second person relation shared by Shakespeare and the Beatles, *me* and *you* not only correspond to the reader or listener and the playwright or singer but negotiate just this universalizing violence ("Et tu, Brute?"). Even in *U,* then, Shakespeare and the Beatles ultimately identify the second-person lyric subject with the ongoing lyric itself, from the play on "a, e, I—o, U [*O, you*]" in Shakespeare's hyperalliterative *Love's Labour's Lost* (5.1.56–57) to the "you are" in "U.S.S.R." ("I'm back in the U.S.S.R. / You don't know how lucky you are [U.R.]") whose larger literalization in the Beatles (cf. "P.S. I Love You [U]" [1962]) probably culminates in "All Together Now" (1967):

    A B C D
    Can I bring my friend to tea [*T*]
    E F G H I J
    I love you [*U*]

In "Back in the U.S.S.R." this lyric *you* transcends postwar popular culture, simultaneously "backing," as McCartney reports of the song's origin in a 1968 "I'm Backing Britain [U.K.]" campaign (Dowlding, 222), the *U.S.* and the *U.S.S.R.:*

    I'm back in the U.S.
    Back in the U.S.
    Back in the U.S.S.R.

Delimiting Cold War popular culture, *you* and *I* alternately back East and West, inside and outside the *system,* from *U.K.* to *Ukraine girls*

("Flew in from Miami Beach B.O.A.C. [*U.S.S.R.*]"). In Lennon's "Revolution," which is also somehow "in" and not "in" the "U.S." and "U.S.S.R." ("But when you talk about destruction / Don't you know that you can count me out—in"), the violence of the "Revolution" is finally inseparable from the mere turning of the record, "out—in out—in," as on the album *Revolver* (1966). At the same popular limit, Shakespeare's plays dialectically refashion the respective courts of Queen Elizabeth and King James. "Whether or not Queen Elizabeth was physically present at the first performance of *A Midsummer Night's Dream*," Montrose observes, "her pervasive *cultural presence* was a condition of the play's imaginative possibilities."[3] From Elizabeth I to Elizabeth II an equally pronounced royal presence pervades the Beatles' album *Abbey Road* (1969), and even the same royal presence, in the case of Lennon's "Mean Mr. Mustard" (Bottom's "Good Master Mustardseed" [3.1.191]):

> Takes him out to look at the Queen
> Only place that he's ever been
> Always shouts out something obscene
> Such a dirty old man.

As in Bottom's working-class relation to Elizabeth in *A Midsummer Night's Dream*, perpetual obedience to the Queen ("Only place that he's ever been") accompanies permanent dissent ("Always shouts out something obscene"). The album concludes with McCartney's "Her Majesty," a song supposedly left by accident at the end of the master tape and thus almost literally on and off the record:

> Her Majesty's a pretty nice girl
> But she doesn't have a lot to say
> Her Majesty's a pretty nice girl
> But she changes from day to day
> I want to tell her that I love her a lot
> But I've got to get a belly full of wine
> Her Majesty's a pretty nice girl
> And some day I'm gonna make her mine.

Once again unquestioned allegiance to the Queen ("I want to tell her that I love her a lot") covers over Bottomesque dissent ("But I've got to get a belly full of wine"); another song on side two of *Abbey Road*, McCartney's "Golden Slumbers," takes the first part of its lyric from the Elizabethan poet Thomas Dekker.

Refiguring one Elizabeth in the other, *Abbey Road* refashions *A Midsummer Night's Dream* in much the way that *Sgt. Pepper* recalls *Julius Caesar* and *Magical Mystery Tour* replays *King Lear*. At either extreme, in turn, the *you* of the lyric is finally the *you*, the reader or listener, of the following refrain from McCartney's "Blackbird" (1968):

> All your life
> You were only waiting for this moment to arise.

The second line is straightforward enough, but its referent is actually double: the antecedent of *arise* is *you*, the blackbird, but it is also *this moment*, as in "the moment arose," freeing up a space for the listener by allowing "You were only waiting for this moment to arise" to make perfect sense even if the *you* is no longer the blackbird. When the refrain is varied later in the lyric to "You were only waiting for this moment to be free," the antecedent of *to be free* is once again both *you* and *this moment*, as in "to have a free moment." If only for a moment, then, "You were only waiting for this moment to be free" addresses a *you* at once inside and outside the lyric; indeed, a follower of Charles Manson actually testified that, among the secret messages "decoded" by Manson from the White Album in the months preceding the Tate–La Bianca murders, "You were only waiting for this moment to arise" convinced him "that the moment was now, that the black man was going to arise, overthrow the white race, and take his turn."[4] Manson's madness is obviously something more than a misdirected manifestation of Beatlemania, but it significantly resonates with the equally extreme rumor of McCartney's death that surfaced in the months following the release of the White Album and that derives from an almost equally pronounced "mania" of interpretation: McCartney's "death" was the subject of several national television specials and the cover of *Life* (6 November 1968). Like the anti-Strat-fordian denunciations of Shakespeare, the rumor resembles Manson not merely because its figural violence depends on an overly scrupu-lous reading of lyrics but because to believe it—namely, that McCart-ney had died in an automobile accident in 1966, a blow to the Beatles but one quickly corrected by the fortunate substitution of one William Shopshire, the winner of a 1965 Paul McCartney look-alike contest, who could also play and write songs like the original—because to believe it one would have to be crazy.

Elsewhere on the White Album this disappearing you of "You were only waiting for this moment to arise" returns to McCartney's other pastoral rhyme of *rise* and *flies* in "Mother Nature's Son," in which "the pretty sound of music" similarly describes both the river and the ongoing song:

Sit beside a mountain stream
See her waters rise
Listen to the pretty sound of music as she flies.

In "The Continuing Story of Bungalow Bill," on the other hand, the Indian backdrop for *A Midsummer Night's Dream* now serves as post-colonial recording studio for a still more imperial Billy Shears:

Deep in the jungle where the mighty tiger hides
Bill and his elephants were taken by surprise
So Captain Marvel zapped him right between the eyes
Zap
All the children sing
Hey Bungalow Bill what did you kill Bungalow Bill
Hey Bungalow Bill wasn't it you Bungalow Bill.⁵

In "Ob-La-Di Ob-La-Da," the song is not just about the song but, like Shakespeare's equally ring-bound *Merchant of Venice*, about its own consumption in the "market place" (Gratiano's closing "Well, while I live I'll fear no other thing / So sore, as keeping safe Nerissa's ring" [5.1.306–7]):

Desmond takes a trolley to the jewelry store
Buys a twenty carat golden ring
Takes it back to Molly waiting at the door
And as he gives it to her she begins to sing
Ob-la-di ob-la-da life goes on.

In line 3 the *it* in "Takes it back to Molly" refers to both the trolley and the ring ("Desmond takes a trolley"); in line 4 *it* names both the ring and the song: "And as he gives it to her she begins to sing / Ob-la-di ob-la-da." Like the *it* in "Sing it again," the object pronoun as the subject of the ongoing song here reaches back to earlier lyrics like the late-recorded and still later released "Come and Get It" (1969/1996), where "If you want it here it is" already glosses over "If you want it *hear* it" ("Did I *hear* you say that there must be a catch [song]"), even as the song winds down on "You better hurry [You better hear it] 'cause it's going fast." In "Ob-La-Di Ob-La-Da" the bawdy innuendo of "as he gives it to her she begins to sing / Ob-la-di Ob-la-da" further confounds the song that is sold and the sex, in this case, that sells:

Happy ever after in the market place
Desmond lets the children lend a hand
Molly stays at home and does her pretty face
And in the evening she still sings it with the band
Ob-la-di ob-la-da life goes on.

The *it* is now the song, but *the band* is still the ring.

Both culturally and personally, the Beatles are thus "Shakespearean" down to the very pun on *beat*, rolling the *ee* of "Beethoven" over the *ea* of "Shakespeare." Even the number 4 for Beatles and 8 of the early film title "Eight Arms to Hold You" refigure the ongoing song in lyrics like "Eight Days a Week" ("Ain't [*eight*] got nothing but love babe"), "Octopus's Garden" ("We would sing and dance around"), "When I'm Sixty-Four" ("Fill in a *form* / Mine *for*ever more"—"You'll be older *too* [*two*]"), "All Together Now" ("One two three four / Can I have a little more"); the thrice repeated four-count that begins Harrison's "Taxman" (1966) further counts out the "Fab Four" alongside the taxman's (and the Beatles') revenues, "one two three four" ("There's *one for you* nineteen *for me*"). Use value, in turn, drops to zero, while exchange value, as Adorno underscores in "The Fetish Character in Music and the Regression of Listening" (1938), zooms to infinity.[6] The hits themselves are "solid gold," Shakespeare crowns "The Golden Age," but that's only because no one would watch a TV show called "Pure Exchange Value." Shakespeare, in turn, delimits early modern culture in part by cross-dressing and unsexing the sexual difference upon which it is grounded, just as, at the same superstructural limit, the Beatles unsettle gender in lyrics like "Sweet Loretta Martin thought she was a woman / But she was another man," "Lovely Rita meter maid / Made her look a little like a military man," "Boy you been a naughty girl you let your knickers down," "Would you love me as much as her," and so on.[7] Thus, in an early song like "Drive My Car" (1965) the car, like the ring, is the song ("I want to be famous / A star of the screen"), and the song is the sex ("But you can do something in between") that sells ("Baby you can drive my car"). The alphabetical opening, "Asked the girl what she wanted to be [*b*] / She said baby can't you see [*c*]," literalizes the *be* in Beatles with the same self-*notation* (the note B then C) that begins "Octopus's Garden"

("I'd like to be / Under the sea"). Autobiographically, then, the pun on "I found a driver and that's a *start*" ("I got no driver and its breaking [*braking*] my heart") continues the sonic play of sex and song ("I told the girl I could start right away") in Lennon's extra-lyric "horny" ("beep beep em beep beep yeah").

Cultural studies, in these terms, returns to Shakespeare and the Beatles in part because the plays and lyrics already record, on the widest possible cultural scale, their own study of culture, from the play-within-the-play in *Hamlet* to the clapping hands, say, throughout "I Want to Hold Your Hand" (1963), which once again refashion the desire in the song as a desire for it. Taking those studies literally, McCartney's "Maxwell's Silver Hammer" (1969) explicitly transforms the postwar university (or *you*-niversity) into postwar Shakespearean drama. For while the lyric typically mingles McCartney (Maxwell), Lennon ("Joan [John] was quizzical"), sexuality ("Late nights all alone with a test tube"), and song ("Bang bang Maxwell's silver hammer came down upon her head"), it also offers its own study in culture every bit as violent as the culture it studies, and therefore every bit as Shakespearean:

> Back in school again
> Maxwell plays the fool again
> Teacher gets annoyed
> Wishing to avoid an unpleasant scene
> She tells Max to stay when the class has gone away
> So he waits behind
> Writing fifty times I must not be so uh oh oh
> But when she turns her back on the boy
> He creeps up from behind
> Bang bang Maxwell's silver hammer came down upon
>   her head
> Bang bang Maxwell's silver hammer made sure that she
>   was dead.

The sonic violence exacted on the teacher ("Bang bang") returns to the listener ("Back in school again"), the one now refigured in the other ("But when she turns her *back* on the boy"). For in "Writing fifty times I must not be so uh oh oh" the lyric *I* (Maxwell) turns lyric *oh* (McCartney) precisely at the moment when the *m* that unites them in *silver hammer* joins the violence performed in the song to the violence it performs ("Bang bang"), like the *m* in "Father McKenzie,"

"Molly [Paulie] Jones [John]," "Lady Madonna" (*Lennon-Mc*Cartney), "Sweet Loretta Martin thought she was a woman" ("Jojo was a man who thought he was a loner"), "Polythene Pam" ("She's so good-looking but she looks like a man"), and so on. In each case a single letter literally divides the authors (Lennon-McCartney) from their subject ("Lady Madonna"). So the more properly Shakespearean *m* of Lennon's decidedly late "Mean Mr. Mustard" much more majestically characterizes McCartney's equally early "Michelle," whose wooing in broken French replays Henry V's halting proposal to Katherine, from "sont des mots qui vont très bien ensemble" to "Le foot et le count! O Seigneur Dieu! ils sont les mots de son mauvais" (3.4.52–53). Thus McCartney's "Paperback Writer" (1966) mingles Lennon the recently published nonsense poet of *In His Own Write* (the chorus of "Frère Jacques" [Brother John] in the background of the final verse), McCartney ("*P*aperback W[*m*]riter"), sexuality ("Dear Sir or Madame"), and song ("If you really like it you can have the rights"), but the lyric also, like "Maxwell's Silver Hammer," significantly recasts *King Lear*, from the "unpleasant scene" in which Maxwell "plays the fool again" to Lennon's emulation of the nonsense poetry of Edward Lear (and *King Lear*) in *In His Own Write* turned "Paperback Writer" ("It's based on a novel by a man named Lear").

From Bungalow Bill, then, to William Shopshire and "the one and only Billy Shears," the difference between Shakespeare and the Beatles, as the shared presence of Julius Caesar suggests, is at once historical, cultural, and literal, like the difference between Shakespeare and Joyce as it culminates in *Ulysses* and *Finnegans Wake:* "our once in only Bragspear, he clanked, to my clinking, from veetoes to threetop, every inch of an immortal" (*FW*, 152.33–34). Shakespeare and the Beatles thus represent powerful cultural markers of a long colonial and postcolonial trajectory, from "With a Little Help from My Friends" back to "Friends, Romans, countrymen, lend me your ears." Bridging these imperial extremes, Billy Shears not only heads up Sgt. Pepper's band but sums up the Beatles in a song written by Lennon for Ringo's debut solo album, "I'm the Greatest" (1973):

Yes my name is Billy Shears
You know it has been for so many years
Now I'm only thirty-two
And all I want to do is boog-a-loo.

Later in the lyric Billy Shears looks back to the Beatles via P. T. Barnum:

I was in the greatest show on earth
For what it was worth
Now I'm only thirty-two
And all I want to do is boog-a-loo.

At the close of *Sgt. Pepper* a similar colonial backdrop for Billy Shears
and "the greatest show on earth" characterizes the Beatles' self-styled
military band in the wake of World War II:

We're Sgt. Pepper's Lonely Hearts Club Band
We hope you have enjoyed the show
Sgt. Pepper's Lonely Hearts Club Band
We're sorry but it's time to go
Sgt. Pepper's Lonely Sgt. Pepper's Lonely
Sgt. Pepper's Lonely Hearts Club Band
We'd like to thank you once again
Sgt. Pepper's one and only Lonely Hearts Club Band
It's getting very near the end
Sgt. Pepper's Lonely Sgt. Pepper's Lonely
Sgt. Pepper's Lonely Hearts Club Band.

As in the chorus to "Eleanor Rigby," "Ah look at all the lonely people," the album ends where it begins, by referring the listener to a
group of people held together by their loneliness, *Eleanor*, again, *Elizabeth*, because *alone* (Lennon [*Eleanor*]–McCartney [*McKenzie*])—the
demon in *Desmond* (*Desdemona*), the *diablo* in *Ob-La-Di* (*Othello*).
More important for the Beatles, such a club, properly managed, must
be joined, since nonmembership is the only condition for belonging.
    Following this final farewell, the encore Lennon-McCartney col-
laboration "A Day in the Life" harkens back to the opening marker of
the irreducible *historicity*, the irreducible temporal distortion and
manipulation, that characterizes music as such: today it was twenty
years ago ("It was twenty years ago—today"):

I read the news today oh boy
About a lucky man who made the grade
And though the news was rather sad
Well I just had to laugh
I saw the photograph

I saw a film today oh boy
The English army had just won the war

A crowd of people turned away
But I just had to look
Having read the book.

With this final written reminder of cultural conquest and the end of
World War II, and with Shakespeare as lead singer, "from me to you,"
across the same centralizing authority embodied by either Elizabeth,
the Beatles thereby literalize, in the largest possible cultural terms,
the psychological and material stresses constitutive of the properly literary tradition, the chiefly lyric tradition, they popularize. As Hunter
Davies observes in his 1985 introduction to *The Beatles* (1968), "the
plays of Shakespeare, the poems of Wordsworth, the novels of Dick-
ens, they have been nurtured into classics. The Beatles were cata-
pulted."[8]

Like the Beatles, then, cultural studies necessarily puts into play
the very culture it sets out to study, creating a hermeneutic circle or
loop that can never quite close, since every closing produces one more
cultural artifact. Every reading, therefore, is also a performance, just
as, in Shakespeare and the Beatles, every performance is also a reading.
The discourse of postmodern cultural studies is thus Shakespearean in
theory because it expresses the same institutional, ideological, and
rhetorical imperatives as the culture it ostensibly explores. For the
various critical paradigms explored in preceding chapters—the new
historicism, psychoanalysis, multiculturalism, feminism, pragmatism, deconstruction, and nuclear criticism—return to Shakespeare
not solely because the postmodern university refashions the early
modern theater but because postmodern culture does. "Cultural criticism," in turn, properly subsumes all forms or schools of postwar criticism, not objectively but subjectively, as specters of the culture they
inspect. In Shakespeare's case such criticism does not so much explain
as expand the poetry and drama, which thereby epitomize or delimit,
from *Beowulf* to the Beatles, postwar literary and cultural criticism.
For *Hamlet* harnesses the tremendous cultural, ideological, and conceptual forces shaping, and shaped by, the national theater, but so, in
a kind of haunting, does the criticism, from the early modern theater
to the postwar, postmodern university.

Notes

Introduction

1. William Shakespeare, *Hamlet,* 1.1.41, in *The Riverside Shakespeare,* ed. G. Blakemore Evans (Boston: Houghton Mifflin, 1974). All citations to Shakespeare (minus editorial brackets) are to this edition.

2. Plato, *The Republic,* from *The Dialogues of Plato,* vol. 1, trans. Benjamin Jowett (New York: Random House, 1937), 377e–78a. All citations to Plato are to this edition, 1974).

3. Steven Mullaney, *The Place of the Stage: License, Play, and Power in Renaissance England* (Chicago: University of Chicago Press, 1988), viii.

4. Leo Strauss, *Socrates and Aristophanes* (Chicago: University of Chicago Press, 1966), 314.

5. Plato, *Republic,* 607b–e; see also Strauss, *Socrates and Aristophanes:* "Aristophanes' presentation of Socrates is the most important document available to us on the ancient disagreement between poetry and philosophy as such—as this feud appears from the side of poetry" (311).

6. Plato, *Apology,* 402 (18d); cf. *Phaedo,* 70b–c.

7. Walter Benjamin, *The Origin of German Tragic Drama,* trans. John Osborne (London: NLB, 1977), 113.

8. Julia Reinhard Lupton and Kenneth Reinhard, *After Oedipus: Shakespeare in Psychoanalysis* (Ithaca: Cornell University Press, 1993), 48. In comments on Plato's allegory of the cave Lupton and Reinhard note how Socrates' passing praise for the stoic shade of Achilles encountered by Odysseus in Hades further superimposes the epic descent of Homer's hero over the philosophical descent of Plato's (31; *Odyssey,* 11.488–91; *Republic,* 7:319).

9. Richard Helgerson, *Forms of Nationhood: The Elizabethan Writing of England* (Chicago: University of Chicago Press, 1992), 203. On this larger Tudor dialogue of theater and university, see Joel Altman, *The Tudor Play of Mind: Rhetorical Inquiry and the Development of Elizabethan Drama* (Berkeley: University of California Press, 1978). Midway between the university playwrights and Shakespeare, Marlowe graduated from Cambridge University in 1587, but only after Elizabeth intervened directly following rumors of German espionage. As Frederick S. Boas notes of *Doctor Faustus*

in *Christopher Marlowe: A Biographical and Critical Study* (Oxford: Oxford University Press, 1940): "Marlowe must have recognized in Faustus his own counterpart. . . . His studies had earned him the Bachelor's and the Master's degrees, but he had turned his back on the Church, and on arrival in London had gained a reputation for atheism. Similarly, Faustus through the bounty of a rich uncle had been sent to Wittenberg to study divinity, and had obtained with credit his doctorate in the subject. But his interests lay elsewhere, and he had turned secretly to the study of necromancy and conjuration" (208).

10. Eleanor Marx-Aveling, "Eleanor Marx on Her Father," in *The Portable Karl Marx*, ed. Eugene Kamenka (New York: Viking, 1983), 50. Originally published as "Karl Marx—Lose Blätter," in *Osterreischer Arbeiter-Kalender für das Jahr 1895*, 51–54.

11. Immanuel Kant, *The Conflict of the Faculties/Der Streit der Fakultäten*, trans. Mary J. Gregory (New York: Abaris Books, 1979), 31; cited in Jacques Derrida, "Mochlos; or, The Conflict of the Faculties," in *Logomachia: The Conflict of the Faculties*, ed. Richard Rand (Lincoln: University of Nebraska Press, 1993), 5.

12. Jacques Derrida, "The Time Is Out of Joint," in *Deconstruction Is/in America: A New Sense of the Political*, ed. Anselm Haverkamp (New York: New York University Press, 1995), 18; Michel Foucault, "Theatrum Philosophicum," in *Language, Counter-Memory, Practice: Selected Essays and an Interview*, ed. Donald F. Bouchard (New York: Cornell University Press, 1977), 165–96; this essay originally appeared in *Critique* 282 (1970): 885–908.

13. Jacques Derrida, *Acts of Literature*, ed. Derek Attridge (New York: Routledge, 1992), 67.

14. Ralph Waldo Emerson, *Representative Men: Seven Lectures*, in *The Complete Works of Ralph Waldo Emerson*, Centenary Edition, 12 vols. (New York: AMS Press, 1968), 204; James Joyce, *Finnegans Wake* (New York: Viking Press, 1959), 177.30–35.

15. Cleanth Brooks, *The Well-Wrought Urn: Studies in the Structure of Poetry* (New York: Harcourt, Brace and Company, 1947), 19.

16. Paul Stevens, "The Political Ways of Paradox: Renaissance Literature and Modern Criticism," *English Literary Renaissance* 26 (Spring 1996): 223.

The Subject of New Historicism

1. Louis Montrose, "The Elizabethan Subject and the Spenserian Text," in *Literary Theory/Renaissance Texts*, ed. Patricia Parker and David Quint (Baltimore: Johns Hopkins University Press, 1986), 305.

2. Louis Montrose, "New Historicisms," in *Redrawing the Boundaries: The Transformation of English and American Literary Studies*, ed. Stephen Greenblatt and Giles Gunn (New York: Modern Language Association of

America, 1992), 415; this passage is again revised in the closing paragraph of Montrose's introduction to *The Purpose of Playing: Shakespeare and the Cultural Politics of the Elizabethan Theatre* (Chicago: University of Chicago Press, 1996): "Integral to any new historicist's project . . ." (16).

3. Stephen Greenblatt, *Learning to Curse: Essays in Early Modern Culture* (New York: Routledge, 1990), 137. The essay first appeared in Parker and Quint, *Literary Theory/Renaissance Texts*, 210–24.

4. See Claude Lévi-Strauss, *Structural Anthropology* (New York: Basic Books, 1963), 201–4; and "A Jivaro Version of *Totem and Taboo*," in *The Jealous Potter*, trans. Benedicte Charier (Chicago: University of Chicago Press, 1988); Jacques Lacan, "Of Structure As an Inmixing of an Otherness Prerequisite to Any Subject Whatever," in *The Structuralist Controversy: The Languages of Criticism and the Sciences of Man*, ed. Richard Macksey and Eugenio Donato (Baltimore: Johns Hopkins University Press, 1972), 189; Jacques Derrida, "Freud and the Scene of Writing," *Writing and Difference*, trans. Alan Bass (Chicago: University of Chicago Press, 1978), 196–231.

5. Louis Montrose, "Professing the Renaissance," in *The New Historicism*, ed. H. Aram Veeser (New York: Routledge, 1989), 18.

6. Greenblatt, *Learning to Curse*, 151–52; Michael Rogin's essay *"Ronald Reagan:* The Movie" first appeared in *democracy* 1 (April and October 1981) and is reprinted with revisions in Rogin's *Ronald Reagan, the Movie and Other Episodes in Political Demonology* (Berkeley: University of California Press, 1987), 1–43.

7. Lars Engle, *Shakespearean Pragmatism: Market of His Time* (Chicago: University of Chicago Press, 1993), 20; italics added.

8. Tobin Siebers, *Cold War Criticism and the Politics of Skepticism* (Oxford: Oxford University Press, 1993), 63.

9. Alan Sinfield, *Faultlines: Cultural Materialism and the Politics of Dissident Reading* (Berkeley: University of California Press, 1992), 290.

10. These quotations are from *Shakespearean Negotiations: The Circulation of Social Energy in Renaissance England* (Berkeley: University of California Press, 1988), 22, 113; *Renaissance Self-Fashioning: From More to Shakespeare* (Chicago: University of Chicago Press, 1980), 252; and *Learning to Curse*, 171.

11. Edgar Allan Poe, "William Wilson," in *The Complete Tales and Poems* (New York: Random House, 1975), 627; cf. Wilson's own double "Will's-son" in the twin *Comedy of Errors* twins of Twain's *Pudd'nhead Wilson*. In Wilson's "among spendthrifts I out-Heroded Herod," the Shakespearean subtext for Wilson's doubling (his out-Heroding Herod) is still more immediately *Hamlet*.

12. Greenblatt, *Learning to Curse*, 139–40; the passage reads "crieds" in the essay's original publication in Parker and Quint, *Literary Theory/Renaissance Texts*, 219.

13. Leah S. Marcus, *Puzzling Shakespeare: Local Reading and Its Discontents* (Berkeley: University of California Press, 1988), 36.

14. Stephen Booth, "On the Value of Hamlet," in *Literary Criticism: Idea and Act,* ed. W. K. Wimsatt (Berkeley: University of California Press, 1974), 297.

Joel Fineman's "Shakespeare's Will"

1. Joel Fineman, "Fratricide and Cuckoldry: Shakespeare's Doubles," in *Representing Shakespeare: New Psychoanalytic Essays,* ed. Murray M. Schwartz and Coppélia Kahn (Baltimore: Johns Hopkins University Press, 1980), 75.

2. Stephen Greenblatt, liner notes to Joel Fineman, *The Subjectivity Effect in Western Literary Tradition: Essays toward the Release of Shakespeare's Will* (Cambridge: MIT Press, 1991); Fineman, *Shakespeare's Will,* 86 n. 34.

3. Fineman, *Shakespeare's Will,* 117.

4. On the play's deconstructive undercurrents, see Jacques Derrida, "Aphorism Countertime," in *Acts of Literature,* 414–33.

5. On Lammas Eve, 31 July, and Juliet, see Barbara Everett, *Young Hamlet: Essays on Shakespeare's Tragedies* (Oxford: Oxford University Press, 1989), 114–15.

6. Joel Fineman: *Shakespeare's Perjured Eye: The Invention of Poetic Subjectivity in the Sonnets* (Berkeley: University of California Press, 1986), 28.

7. Sigmund Freud, "The Theme of the Three Caskets," in *The Standard Edition of the Complete Psychological Works of Sigmund Freud,* vol. 12, ed. James Strachey (London: Hogarth Press, 1958), 296–300.

8. Herbert Blau, *Take Up the Bodies: Theater at the Vanishing Point* (Urbana: University of Illinois Press, 1982), 93.

9. Johannes Birringer, *Theatre, Theory, Postmodernism* (Bloomington: Indiana University Press, 1991), 90.

10. Ned Lukacher, *Primal Scenes: Literature, Philosophy, Psychoanalysis* (Ithaca: Cornell University Press, 1986), 225, 198.

11. Ned Lukacher, *Daemonic Figures: Shakespeare and the Question of Conscience* (Ithaca: Cornell University Press, 1994), 7, 147, 94.

12. Jacques Lacan, "Desire and the Interpretation of Desire in *Hamlet,*" in *Literature and Psychoanalysis: The Question of Reading: Otherwise,* ed. Shoshana Felman (Baltimore: Johns Hopkins University Press, 1982), 47–48.

13. Daniel Sibony, *"Hamlet: A Writing Effect,"* in *Literature and Psychoanalysis,* 61–62.

14. Jean-Luc Nancy and Philippe Lacoue-Labarthe, *The Title of the Letter: A Reading of Lacan* (Albany: SUNY Press, 1992), 108; Jacques Lacan, "Lituraterre," *Littérature,* no. 3 (1971): 3–10.

15. On *mother* and *matter* in *Hamlet,* see also James W. Stone, "Androgynous 'Union' and the Woman in *Hamlet,*" *Shakespeare Studies* 23 (1995): 72.

16. Sandra M. Gilbert and Susan Gubar, "Masterpiece Theatre: An Academic Melodrama," *Critical Inquiry* 17 (Summer 1991): 701.

17. Leo Lowenthal, "Memorial," *Representations* 28 (Fall 1989): 5.

The Place of the University: Shakespeare and Multiculturalism

1. David Rieff, "Multiculturalism's Silent Partner: It's the Newly Globalized Consumer Economy, Stupid," *Harper's*, August 1993, 63.

2. David Lodge, *After Bakhtin: Essays on Fiction and Criticism* (New York: Routledge, 1990), 178. Regarding deconstruction's inside-outside relation to "political correctness," Peggy Kamuf observes in "Going Public: The University in Deconstruction": "The fact that deconstruction can be positioned as at once too political and not political at all, as both PC and not PC, signals that the terms in which the political is posed in this debate are inadequate to account for all the effects being produced" (in *Deconstruction Is/in America*, 110).

3. Louis Althusser, "Ideology and Ideological State Apparatuses (Notes toward an Investigation)," in *Lenin and Philosophy and Other Essays*, trans. Ben Brewster (New York: Monthly Review Press, 1972), 175.

4. Karl Mannheim, *Ideology and Utopia: An Introduction to the Sociology of Knowledge*, trans. Louis Wirth and Edward Shils (New York: Harcourt, 1936), 277.

5. Richard Levin, "Feminist Thematics and Shakespearean Tragedy," *PMLA* (March 1988): 125.

6. *PMLA* (January 1989): 77.

7. Gerald Graff, *Beyond the Culture Wars* (New York: Norton, 1992), 38–39.

8. Peter Erickson, *Rewriting Shakespeare, Rewriting Ourselves* (New York: Routledge, 1991), 5.

9. Stephen Booth, *Shakespeare's Sonnets* (New Haven: Yale University Press, 1977), 346.

10. Immanuel Kant, *The Conflict of the Faculties, 57;* as cited (and translated) in Pierre Bourdieu, *Homo Academicus*, trans. Peter Collier (Stanford: Stanford University Press, 1988), 36.

11. Sacvan Bercovitch, *The Rites of Assent: Transformations in the Symbolic Construction of America* (New York: Routledge, 1993), 373.

12. Ellen Rooney, *Seductive Reasoning: Pluralism as the Problematic of Contemporary Literary Theory* (Ithaca: Cornell University Press, 1989), 18–19.

13. Jean Howard, "Scholarship, Theory, and More New Readings: Shakespeare for the 1990s," in *Shakespeare Study Today: The Horace Howard Furness Memorial Lectures*, ed. Georgianna Ziegler (New York: AMS Press, 1986), 146.

Feminism and Theater in The Taming of the Shrew

1. See Harold Goddard, *The Meaning of Shakespeare,* vol. 1 (Chicago: University of Chicago Press, 1951), 65–68.

2. On the Lord's "twenty pound" and Petruchio's "Twenty crowns," see Dorothea Kehler, "Echoes of the Induction in *The Taming of the Shrew,*" *Renaissance Papers* (1986): 36, 39; and Margie Burns, "The Ending of the Shrew," *Shakespeare Studies* 18 (1986): 45. According to Kehler, "The precision of this second echo makes unmistakable the significant thematic link between the Induction and the play proper, delineating the action of taming at its most crass" (40). Burns mentions the actor Will Sly and his possible relation to the character Christopher Sly in a note (63 n. 20). On the names Christopher and Katherine, see Laurie E. Maguire, "'Household Kates': Chez Petruchio, Percy and Plantagenet," in *Gloriana's Face: Women, Public and Private, in the English Renaissance,* ed. S. P. Cerasano and Marion Wynne-Davies (Detroit: Wayne State University, 1992), 131–33.

3. As Thomas Moisan observes of Bianca's Latin lesson on old Priam turned gulled Baptista, "the translation scene epitomizes the uses, or misuses, to which education and formal 'learning' are put throughout the play, with educational projects and the value of learning invoked only to be genially disregarded, subordinated to other plans, or simply, and just as genially, trashed, the ridicule to which they are subjected personified in the stock figure of the hapless, and perhaps spurious, 'Pedant' who fecklessly wanders into the play in time to provide fodder for one of the 'wily servant' Tranio's schemes" ("Interlinear Trysting and 'Household Stuff': The Latin Lesson and the Domestication of Learning in *The Taming of the Shrew,*" *Shakespeare Studies* 23 [1995]: 103–4).

4. Miguel de Cervantes, *Don Quixote,* trans. J. M. Cohen (New York: Penguin, 1950), 75.

5. In Joyce's *Ulysses* Stephen Dedalus offers an autobiographical reading of *The Taming of the Shrew* that might be further supported by the Induction's various allusions to Stratford, citizens then living in Stratford, and the environs—the notorious "Ann hath-a-way," following sonnet 145's "I hate from *hate away* she threw, / And saved my life saying, 'not you,'" in "Burton Heath" (Ind.2.18) and "Marian Hacket" (21–22); James Joyce, *Ulysses* (New York: Random House, 1986), 157; Booth, *Shakespeare's Sonnets,* 501.

6. Herbert A. Ellis, *Shakespeare's Lusty Punning in* Love's Labour's Lost (The Hague: Mouton, 1973), 164. Ellis suggests a possible further play on *more L, moral,* and *morall,* a phallic mushroom.

7. Both *Love's Labour's Lost* and *The Taming of the Shrew,* in this regard, are closer still to *A Midsummer Night's Dream,* which ends rather than begins with the problematic taming of its Amazonian Dian—Grumio's "Katherine the curst [Elizabeth the First]" (1.2.129). The seasonal difference superimposed over the play's battle of the sexes (Kate's "It blots thy beauty, as frosts do bite the meads" [5.2.139]) further underwrites Titania's "And

thorough this distemperature, we see / The seasons alter: hoary-headed frosts / Fall in the fresh lap of the crimson rose" (2.1.106–8).

8. The moral Pandarus draws, that the play has now subsumed the sexual difference around which it is written and may therefore end, further recalls, from *Full* to *fail*, the *more L* of *Love's Labour's Lost:* "What verse for it? What instance for it? Let me see:

> Full merrily the humble-bee doth sing,
> Till he hath lost his honey and his sting;
> And being once subdued in armed tail,
> Sweet honey and sweet notes together fail."

(5.10.40–44)

9. An earlier version of this chapter was presented under the title "The Shaming of the True" as part of a seminar organized by Barbara Freedman for the 1992 Shakespeare Association of America convention. My thanks to her and other conference participants for helpful suggestions.

10. Nevill Coghill, "The Basis of Shakespearean Comedy," *Essays and Studies* (1950): 11. See Margaret Webster, *Shakespeare without Tears* (New York: McGraw-Hill, 1942), 142. It was Webster's great-grandfather Ben Webster who in 1844 first restored Shakespeare's original *Taming of the Shrew* after David Garrick's shorter and simpler version had held the stage for ninety years; see Webster's "Director's Comments" in Tori Haring-Smith, *From Farce to Melodrama: A Stage History of* The Taming of the Shrew (Westport, Conn.: Greenwood Press, 1985), 44–45.

11. I consider the special place of Poe's "Purloined Letter" in the theater-theory continuum set forth here in "The Figure-Power Dialectic: Poe's 'Purloined Letter,'" *MLN* 110 (September 1995): 679–91.

12. Richard Hosley, "Introduction" to the Pelican edition of *The Taming of the Shrew* (Penguin: Baltimore, 1964), 16. Coppélia Kahn, "*The Taming of the Shrew:* Shakespeare's Mirror of Marriage," *Modern Language Studies* 5 (Spring 1975): 89; reprinted in *The Authority of Experience: Essays in Feminist Criticism,* ed. Lee Edwards and Arlyn Diamond (Amherst: University of Massachusetts Press, 1976). This essay, revised as part of "Coming of Age: Marriage and Manhood in *Romeo and Juliet* and *The Taming of the Shrew,*" appears in Kahn, *Man's Estate: Masculine Identity in Shakespeare* (Berkeley: University of California Press, 1981): "in the last scene, Shakespeare finally allows Petruchio that lordship over Kate and superiority to other husbands for which he has striven so mightily. He just makes it clear to us, through the contextual irony of Kate's last speech, that his mastery is an illusion" (114). Roger L. Cox, *Shakespeare's Comic Changes: The Time-Lapse Metaphor as Plot Device* (Athens: University of Georgia Press, 1991), 61–62.

13. Robert B. Heilman, "*The Taming* Untamed, or, The Return of the Shrew," *Modern Language Quarterly* 27 (1966): 151.

14. Richard Levin, *New Readings vs. Old Plays: Recent Trends in the Reinterpretation of English Renaissance Drama* (Chicago: University of Chicago Press, 1979), 134; Peter Saccio, "Shrewd and Kindly Farce," *Shakespeare Quarterly* 37 (1984): 39; Camille Wells Slights, *Shakespeare's Comic Commonwealths* (Toronto: University of Toronto Press, 1993), 52.

15. Jonathan Hall, *Anxious Pleasures: Shakespearean Comedy and the Nation-State* (Madison: Farleigh Dickinson University Press, 1995), 158; Natasha Korda, "Household Kates: Domesticating Commodities in *The Taming of the Shrew,*" *Shakespeare Quarterly* 47 (Summer 1996): 130–31.

16. Karen Newman, *Fashioning Femininity and English Renaissance Drama* (Chicago: University of Chicago Press, 1991), 42.

17. Valerie Traub, *Desire and Anxiety: Circulations of Sexuality in Shakespearean Drama* (New York: Routledge, 1992), 17.

18. Barbara Freedman, *Staging the Gaze: Postmodernism, Psychoanalysis, and Shakespearean Comedy* (Ithaca: Cornell University Press, 1991), 146.

19. Jean E. Howard, *The Stage and Social Struggle in Early Modern England* (New York: Routledge, 1994), 44.

20. Fineman, *Shakespeare's Will,* 139.

21. Michel Foucault, *The History of Sexuality,* vol. 1, trans. Robert Hurley (New York: Random House, 1990), 103.

22. Sue-Ellen Case, *Feminism and Theater* (New York: Methuen, 1988), 12.

The Pragmatist Dilemma: Henry V

1. Richard Rorty, *Contingency, Irony, Solidarity* (Cambridge: Cambridge University Press, 1989), 20.

2. Terence Hawkes, *Meaning by Shakespeare* (New York: Routledge, 1992), 8.

3. Herman Melville, *Moby-Dick* (New York: Norton Critical Edition, 1967), 480.

4. Jorge Luis Borges, *Labyrinths,* trans. James E. Irby (New York: New Directions, 1964), 73–74.

5. Cited in Albert Furtwangler, *Assassins on Stage: Brutus, Hamlet, and the Death of Lincoln* (Urbana: University of Illinois Press, 1991), 71.

6. René Girard, *A Theater of Envy* (New York: Oxford University Press, 1991), 200–226; and *Violence and the Sacred,* trans. P. Gregory (Baltimore: Johns Hopkins University Press, 1977).

7. Gerald Gould, "A New Reading of *Henry V,*" *English Review* 29 (1919): 42–55; reprinted in *Shakespeare:* Henry V. *A Casebook,* ed. M. Quinn (London: Macmillan, 1969), 81–94; Norman Rabkin, *Shakespeare and the Problem of Meaning* (Chicago: University of Chicago Press, 1981), 33–62. A century before Gould's comments, and in a corresponding climate of post-Napoleonic historical jadedness, William Hazlitt refers to Henry as a "most

amiable monster" (*Characters of Shakespeare's Plays* [New York: E. P. Dutton, 1926], 158): "The object of our late invasion and conquest of France was to restore the legitimate monarch, the descendant of Hugh Capet, to the throne; Henry V, in his time, made war on and deposed the descendant of this very Hugh Capet, on the plea that he was a usurper and illegitimate" (157).

8. David Quint, "'Alexander the Pig': Shakespeare on History and Poetry," in *Modern Critical Interpretations: Shakespeare's* Henry V, ed. Harold Bloom (New York: Chelsea House, 1988), 75.

9. Here "the general" further situates the play's notorious loss of difference or degree within the culturally empowering difference between Agamemnon (the general) and his army ("the general" of Hamlet's roughly contemporary "'twas caviary to the. general" [2.2.457], this of a speech recounting Troy's fall, but also of Claudius's "the great love the general gender bear him" [4.7.18], which more nearly approximates "the general sex"):

> When that the general is not like the hive,
> To whom the foragers shall all repair,
> What honey is expected?
>
> (1.3.81–83)

In *The Riverside Shakespeare* G. Blakemore Evans glosses "like the hive" as follows: "i.e., the centre to which all energy is directed and from which all order emanates. The bee-state analogy was a favorite with the Elizabethans; cf. *Henry V*, I.ii.187–204." But *the general* may also refer to the hive-like army (rather than Agamemnon) and *the foragers* to temporary dissidents from that assemblage (the moral, again, of the bee-state analogy in *Henry V*). That Essex in *Troilus and Cressida* should be identified by critics with both Achilles and Hector deepens the play's pragmatic transposition of contemporary historical violence, a give-and-take of literature and history that probably culminates in Essex's own "non-commissioned" *Richard II* on the eve of his failed rebellion; on Essex, Hector, and Achilles, see Eric Mallin, "Emulous Factions and the Collapse of Chivalry: *Troilus and Cressida*, *Representations* 29 (Winter 1990): 145–79.

10. Jonathan Goldberg, *Sodometries: Renaissance Texts, Modern Sexualities* (Stanford: Stanford University Press, 1992), 5.

11. For a parallel co-opting of resistance within Elizabethan politics as played out in *Henry V*, see Greenblatt, *Shakespearean Negotiations*, 40–65.

12. Cornel West, *The American Evasion of Philosophy: A Genealogy of Pragmatism* (Madison: University of Wisconsin Press, 1989), 5.

13. On Williams and Shakespeare, see Phyllis Rackin, *Stages of History: Shakespeare's English Chronicles* (Ithaca: Cornell University Press, 1990), 243–44.

14. Richard's opening lines also reach *back* in time to Kyd's *Spanish Tragedy*: "But in the harvest of my summer joys / Death's winter nipped the blossoms of my bliss" (1.1.12–13).

15. Stanley Fish, *Is There a Text in This Class? The Authority of Interpretive Communities* (Cambridge: Harvard University Press, 1980), 244.

16. Gary Wihl, *The Contingency of Theory: Pragmatism, Expressivism, and Deconstruction* (New Haven: Yale University Press, 1994), 131; see Terry Eagleton, *Ideology: An Introduction* (London: Verso, 1991), 172–73, 202.

17. Michael Goldman, *Shakespeare and the Energies of Drama* (Princeton: Princeton University Press, 1972), 57. For Harry Berger Jr. "the success of spectator and soldier alike depends on force of imaginative thought. As the spectator's imagination succeeds, he becomes the soldier. And since every spectator is in reality a potential English soldier, the play claims to be a kind of war game, a patriotic exercise carried on within the modest and relatively humble 'girdle of these walls'" (*Second World and Green World: Studies in Renaissance Fiction-Making* [Berkeley: University of California Press, 1988], 131).

"By heaven, thou echoest me": Lentricchia, Othello, *de Man*

1. Stephen Booth, "The Audience as Malvolio," in *Shakespeare's "Rough Magic": Renaissance Essays in Honor of C. L. Barber,* ed. Peter Erickson and Coppélia Kahn (Newark: University of Delaware Press, 1985). This chapter on *Othello* and de Man appeared in the journal *Diacritics* just prior to the discovery of de Man's wartime journalism in 1987; the next chapter was published in the book of *Responses* to those same writings.

2. Stanley Cavell, *Disowning Knowledge in Six Plays of Shakespeare,* 162–68.

3. Joel Fineman, "Fratricide and Cuckoldry," 86.

4. Frank Lentricchia, *Criticism and Social Change* (Chicago: University of Chicago Press, 1983), 163; hereafter cited in the text by page number.

5. Frank Lentricchia, *After the New Criticism* (Chicago: University of Chicago Press, 1980), 298.

6. The words Lentricchia quotes here are de Man's, but this is precisely the point.

7. Kenneth Burke, "*Othello:* An Essay to Illustrate a Method," *Hudson Review* 4 (1951): 202.

8. F. R. Leavis, *The Common Pursuit* (New York: New York University Press, 1952), 140–41. Leavis's chapter on *Othello*, "Diabolic Intellect and the Noble Hero," was first published in *Scrutiny* 6 (1937): 250–71.

9. On Macbeth, the Medusa, and the theatrical gaze, see D. J. Palmer, "A New Gorgon: Visual Effects in *Macbeth*," in *Focus on* Macbeth, ed. John Russell Brown (London: Routledge, 1982), 54–69.

10. On de Man and the Medusa, see also Jonathan Arac, *Critical Genealogies: Historical Situations for Postmodern Literary Studies* (New York: Columbia University Press, 1987), 108.

11. Greenblatt, *Renaissance Self-Fashioning,* 233.

Synchronic Theory and Absolutism: "Et tu, Brute?"

1. Paul de Man, *Allegories of Reading: Figural Language in Rousseau, Rilke, and Proust* (New Haven: Yale University Press, 1979), 78; hereafter cited in the text as *AR*; on de Man's "Hamlet-like" detachment, see Christopher Norris, *Paul de Man: Deconstruction and the Critique of Aesthetic Ideology* (New York: Routledge, 1988), 16.

2. John Fekete, *The Critical Twilight: Explorations in the Ideology of Anglo-American Literary Theory from Eliot to McLuhan* (London: Routledge, 1977). For de Man's "quietism," see Frank Lentricchia, *Criticism and Social Change*, 51.

3. Jacques Derrida, *Margins of Philosophy*, trans. Alan Bass (Chicago: University of Chicago Press, 1982), 5.

4. Ferdinand de Saussure, *Course in General Linguistics*, trans. Wade Baskin (New York: McGraw-Hill, 1959), 120.

5. Paul de Man, *The Resistance to Theory* (Minneapolis: University of Minnesota Press, 1986), 8; hereafter cited in the text as *RT*.

6. Roman Jakobson, "Linguistics and Poetics," in *Style in Language*, ed. Thomas A. Sebeok (Cambridge, Mass.: MIT Press, 1960), 89.

7. It is interesting to note that the title of both of these autobiographies is seldom translated. This is in fact one effect of the textual authority we are considering here.

8. *Après coup* was completed early in 1941, when Henri de Man was still in Belgium and still vaguely optimistic about his vision of a socialist Europe: "Maintenant, à la fin de l'hiver de guerre où j'ai écrit ce livre, je puis dire, comme le spectre de Hamlet: 'Il me semble que je hume l'air du matin'—même sans être sur si je verrai encore se dissiper les ténèbres" (Brussels: Editions de la Toison d'Or, 1941), 322.

9. Paul de Man, *The Rhetoric of Romanticism* (New York: Columbia University Press, 1984), 242.

10. Paul de Man, *Blindness and Insight* (Minneapolis: University of Minnesota Press, 1983 [1971]), 165.

11. The exception, of course, is *King Lear*, both regarding Caesar, whom the action of the play precedes, and its conspicuous lack of closure.

12. The hostess here describes Falstaff thus.

13. Hélène Cixous and Catherine Clément, *The Newly Born Woman*, trans. Betsy Wing (Minneapolis: University of Minnesota Press, 1986), 124–25.

14. On Freud, *Hamlet*, and Vienna, see Sibony, 61.

15. Karl Marx, *Der achtzehnte Brumaire des Louis Bonaparte* (Leipzig: Dietz Verlag, 1984), 128, 21; translation follows *The Portable Karl Marx*, ed. Eugene Kamenka (New York: Penguin, 1983), 289–90. On Hamlet and Marx's *Eighteenth Brumaire of Louis Bonaparte*, see Lukacher, *Primal Scenes*, 236–74.

16. For an interesting account of variant readings given Shakespeare's

Caesar, see Ernest Schanzer, *The Problem Plays of Shakespeare* (New York: Schocken Books, 1963), 32 ff.

17. This warning is spoken in soliloquy by Artemidorus of Cnidos, identified in the dramatis personae of the First Folio as "a teacher of rhetoric."

18. An interesting parallel to de Man's wartime writings is provided by the discovery of a pro-Nazi review published by Adorno in June 1934 in *Die Musik*, "the official journal for the direction of the youth of the Reich." In a note in *La Fiction du politique* (Paris: Christian Bourgois, 1987), Philippe Lacoue-Labarthe summarizes the events surrounding an open letter to Adorno published in the Frankfurt student journal in January of 1963, inquiring whether he was the author of the review and asking how he could thus condemn all those complicit in the development of Germany beginning from 1934, particularly Heidegger. In response, Adorno acknowledged authorship and expressed his regret. But he also asked whether, in the scales of an "equitable justice," the review presented "a very great weight in comparison to my work and to my life." On the question of Heidegger, he writes: "Concerning the continuity of my work, it should not be permitted to compare me to Heidegger, whose philosophy is fascist down to its innermost cells [*dessen Philosophie bis in ihre innersten Zellen faschistisch ist*]." Of this response, Lacoue-Labarthe notes, Hannah Arendt wrote to Karl Jaspers on July 4, 1966 that she found it "'indescribably distressing.'" Adorno's letter is reprinted in an afterword to *Musikalische Schriften* (Frankfurt: Suhrkamp, 1984), 6:637–38. My thanks to Jonathan Culler for drawing this to my attention and for many helpful suggestions elsewhere.

19. Theodor Adorno, "Commitment," in *The Essential Frankfurt School Reader*, ed. Andrew Arato and Eike Gebhardt (New York: Continuum Publishing Company, 1987), 301; hereafter cited in the text as CM.

Nuclear Criticism (the Aufhebung of the Sun)

1. René Girard, *A Theater of Envy* (Oxford: Oxford University Press, 1991), 286.

2. See Greg Herken, *The Winning Weapon: The Atomic Bomb in the Cold War: 1945–50* (New York: Knopf, 1980), 20–21.

3. Ken Ruthven, *Nuclear Criticism* (Carlton, Victoria: Melbourne University Press, 1993), 34.

4. Jacques Derrida, "Two Words for Joyce," in *Post-structuralist Joyce*, ed. Derek Attridge and Daniel Ferrer (Cambridge: Cambridge University Press, 1984), 147.

5. Derrida, *Acts of Literature*, 418–19.

6. Fineman, *Shakespeare's Perjured Eye*, 128–29.

7. Howard Felperin, *Beyond Deconstruction: The Uses and Abuses of Literary Theory* (Oxford: Oxford University Press, 1985), 189–90.

8. Jacques Derrida, "No Apocalypse, Not Now (full speed ahead, seven missiles, seven missives)" (*Diacritics* 14, no. 2, ed. Richard Klein [Summer 1984]: 27).

9. Nathaniel Hawthorne, *The House of the Seven Gables* (New York: Signet Classic, 1961), 144.

10. Paul de Man, *Allegories of Reading*, 298; Herman Melville, *Billy Budd and Other Stories* (New York: Penguin, 1986), 279.

11. Thomas Pynchon, *Gravity's Rainbow* (New York: Viking, 1973). For the Pynchon-Hawthorne relation, see Mathew Winston's "The Quest for Pynchon," in *Twentieth Century Literature* 21 (October 1975). My thanks to Seiji Lippit for drawing this to my attention.

12. Floyd Merrell, *Deconstruction Reframed* (West Lafayette, Ind.: Purdue University Press, 1985); Gregory L. Ulmer, *Applied Grammatology: Post(e) Pedagogy from Jacques Derrida to Joseph Beuys* (Baltimore: Johns Hopkins University Press, 1985).

13. Jacques Derrida, *Margins of Philosophy*, xxiii.

14. Jacques Derrida, "Fors," trans. Barbara Johnson, *Georgia Review* 31 (1977).

15. Jacques Derrida, *Speech and Phenomena,* trans. David B. Allison (Evanston: Northwestern University Press, 1973), 143, 140, 148; Derrida's comments on "the Einsteinian constant" come in response to a question from Jean Hippolyte following a reading of Derrida's essay "Structure, Sign, and Play in the Discourse of the Human Sciences," in *The Structuralist Controversy,* 267.

16. Jacques Derrida, *Writing and Difference,* 17; *Margins,* 251; Ulmer, *Applied Grammatology,* 86.

17. Frances Ferguson, "The Nuclear Sublime," *Diacritics* (Summer 1984): 4–10.

18. Paul de Man, "Hegel on the Sublime," in *Displacement: Derrida and After,* ed. Mark Krupnik (Bloomington: Indiana University Press, 1983), 146.

19. Neil Hertz, *The End of the Line: Essays on Psychoanalysis and the Sublime* (New York: Columbia University Press, 1985), 3.

20. Jacques Derrida, "Biodegradables: Seven Diary Fragments," *Critical Inquiry* (Summer 1989): 861.

21. Jacques Derrida, *Writing and Difference,* 17.

Cultural Studies: Shakespeare and the Beatles

1. All Beatles lyrics are reprinted from Colin Campbell and Allan Murphy, ed., *Things We Said Today: The Complete Lyrics and a Concordance to the Beatles* (Ann Arbor: Pierian Press, 1980). On the unprecedented praise afforded *Sgt. Pepper,* see William J. Dowlding, *Beatlesongs* (New York: Simon and Schuster, 1989), 161–63.

2. *Rolling Stone,* 31 January 1974; see Dowlding, *Beatlesongs,* 164.

3. Louis Montrose, "'Shaping Fantasies': Figurations of Gender and Power

in Elizabethan Culture," *Representations* 1 (Spring 1983): 32; see also Annabel Patterson, "Bottoms Up: Festive Theory," in her book *Shakespeare and the Popular Voice* (Cambridge, Mass.: Basil Blackwell, 1989), 52–70.

4. Vincent Bugliosi, *Helter Skelter* (New York: Norton, 1974), 326.

5. According to Lennon, the name Bungalow Bill conflates Jungle Jim and Buffalo Bill. Of the song's genesis, he remarks: "That was written about a guy in Maharishi's meditation camp who took a short break to shoot a few tigers, and then came back to commune with God" (David Shieff and G. Barry Golson, *The Playboy Interviews with John Lennon and Yoko Ono* [New York: Berkeley Books, 1981]; cited in Dowlding, *Beatlesongs*, 228).

6. Adorno later expanded on this essay in a chapter on "The Culture Industry: Enlightenment as Mass Deception" in *The Dialectic of Enlightenment*, with Max Horkheimer (New York: Continuum, 1972), 120–67.

7. These lyrics are from "Get Back" (1969), "Lovely Rita Meter Maid" (1967), "I Am the Walrus," and "If I Fell" (1964).

8. Hunter Davies, *The Beatles* (New York: McGraw-Hill, 1968), x.

Index